BASIC FOR THE DEC10

Irmtraud Seeborg
Cynthia Ma

Ball State University

Engineering Press, Inc. San Jose, California 95103-0001

Library of Congress Cataloging in Publication Data

Seeborg, Irmtraud, 1939-
Basic for the DEC-10.

Includes index.
1. Basic (Computer program language)
2. DECsystem-10 (Computer) - -Programming. I. Ma, Cynthia, 1938- II. Title.
QA76.73.B3S4 1982 001.64'24 82-13957
ISBN 0-910554-37-4

Printed in the United States of America

Engineering Press, Inc. P.O. Box 1 San Jose, California 95103-0001

Contents

1

Introduction

1.1 Use of Computers in Engineering

In engineering textbooks that were written a decade or two ago, a chapter was sometimes devoted to the use of computers, pointing out that computers were fast becoming a tool to aid the engineer in solving a variety of problems.

With the development of computer technology in the past decade, the computer has become a frequently used tool not only for engineers, but even for students in their early college or high school years. The application possibilities have increased so much it would be difficult to number them all. In addition to straight computational usage — solving of equations, analyzing large sets of data — the computer is used for simulating real-life situations to aid in decision-making, for data storage and retrieval, for drafting, and for controlling industrial processes, to name but a few. Many of these applications use the computer in an interactive mode — the user "converses" with the computer, receives immediate responses and can provide additional information and corrections.

A prerequisite for using the computer is the ability to communicate with it — to learn a programming language. A number of languages are available. They have often been developed with specific applications in mind such as business applications (COBOL) or scientific applications (FORTRAN).

The purpose of this text is to introduce the reader to a language that is easy to use, can be learned in a short period of time, and allows the user to solve a variety of problems — BASIC (Beginners All-Purpose

Symbolic Instruction Code). BASIC was created for time-sharing computer users by Professors J. G. Kemeny and T. E. Kurtz at Dartmouth College. It uses a combination of ordinary English words and familiar algebraic symbols and operates in a real-time environment. In section 1.5, an example of a BASIC program is shown; line 10 illustrates one of the interactive features, the diagnosis of errors as soon as a line is typed in.

In the remaining sections of this chapter, the reader will receive a very general introduction to the use of the DEC10 and BASIC. A sample program will be given and explained. A detailed explanation of the statements and logic of BASIC programs will be the topic of the remaining chapters.

1.2 Basic Concepts

A computer system has a number of components. For our understanding of BASIC programming, we need to be familiar with the following terms: *Core* or memory is the part of the computer where programs and data can be stored temporarily and from which programs can be executed. As soon as the user terminates communication with the computer, all information in core is lost.

Disk is a permanent storage device. Information can be transferred from core to disk and from disk to core. Each user has a designated disk area available. The user is given a PPN (project — programmer number) which is used to control access to the computer and to identify the disk area. Information stored on disk remains available unless it is deleted by the user.

A *program* is a set of instructions for the computer. Programs are written in specific programming languages; one of these languages is BASIC. Each programming language has a specific vocabulary and syntax. Individual statements are combined into a program; the program is translated by a compiler into machine language. The machine language program is then executed.

Programs can be stored on disk. They are given a name so that they can be retrieved; this name is known as filename and the area on the disk in which the program is stored is referred to as a *file*. On the DEC10, filenames can have up to six characters and letters with a 3-letter extension. An example of a filename is

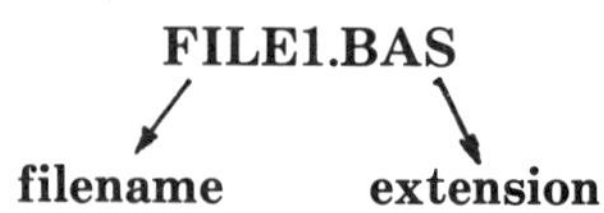

Information can be entered into the computer in various ways. In this manual, it is assumed that information (both programs and

data) are entered from a terminal. This allows the user to interact with the program, as will be illustrated in the next section.

In the remaining sections of this chapter, some basic steps in the creation of a BASIC program will be discussed — LOGIN procedures, monitor commands, and debugging a program. An example is given in section 1.3, but the BASIC statements used in the example will be discussed later in the book and are not explained at this point.

1.3 LOGIN Procedures[1]

BASIC is designed for interactive use — one can sit down at the terminal, enter the program, execute it, make necessary corrections, and obtain the output all in one session. The following steps are necessary for a complete session with the DEC-10:

1. If the terminal is a dial-up terminal, call to connect the terminal to the computer; in many cases, the terminal is permanently connected to the system, and this step is not necessary. It may be necessary to turn on the power.
2. Type LOGIN followed by your PPN, for example:

   LOGIN 10101,10001

   The computer will respond with some identifying information, for example:

   JOB 23 BALL STATE 6.02 KL (01)TTY19

   Each job that is running at a given time has a unique job number which is assigned at LOGIN time. TTY19 identifies the terminal on which the LOGIN was typed.
3. After giving the information above, the word PASSWORD is typed by the system. The user responds by typing in his password and pressing the carriage return. The password will not be shown on the terminal; it is known only to the user and the system to protect the user's files and, possibly, budget.

   If the correct password is given, the time of day, the date, and possibly a number of messages are typed. This communication ends with a period at the beginning of a line. The computer is now ready to accept the user's commands.
4. At this time, a program called monitor is in core. To enter a BASIC program, the BASIC compiler has to be loaded into

[1] These may vary from system to system; check with your computer center for possible deviations from the procedure outlined here.

memory. Thus, the next step is to type R BASIC, followed by a carriage return. Note: Each command ends with a carriage return; without it, the command will not be executed.

5. After the BASIC compiler is loaded into memory, it types

   READY, FOR HELP TYPE HELP

   If the user types HELP, a list of BASIC commands and their functions will be produced. It is, however, not necessary to type HELP.

   At this point, the user's program can be typed in. It will be explained in later chapters how to write a BASIC program; in figure 1-1, an example of such a program is shown. The filename PROGR.BAS was assigned by the user; any other name of legal length would have been equally appropriate.

6. After the program has been typed in, the word RUN is typed. This causes the program to be executed.
7. If mistakes are detected in the program, error messages will be printed (see section 1-5 on debugging). Otherwise, the output produced by the program execution will be printed if the program so specifies (see figure 1-1). The word READY at the end is a sign that the computer is ready for additional commands. Available commands are discussed in section 1-4.
8. After all the desired work has been accomplished, the user signs off the system by typing BYE. Figure 1-1 shows the information provided at this time.

1.4 BASIC Commands

Figure 1-1 shows two types of instructions that can be given to the computer — commands and statements. Statements can be identified through the statement number at the beginning of the line. Statements 10 through 50 form a BASIC program. Commands are *not* part of a program; instead they operate on an entire program. Commands have no line numbers and typically consist of a short English word and a file name. NEW, RUN, and BYE in figure 1-1 are examples of commands. When a command has been executed, the word READY is typed, indicating that you may issue another command. In this section we will discuss some of the commands that are necessary to create, run, and store a program in BASIC.

1.4.1 Creating a Program File — NEW

The first step to create a new program is to clear core (in case a prior program is still stored) and to assign a name to the program. The

```
 LOGIN 10101,1
JOB 17 BALL STATE 6.03A KL (13) TTY10
Password:
1005                     Mon

.R BASIC


Ready, for help type HELP.
NEW
New file name--FIG11.BAS

Ready
10 READ A,B,C
20 DATA 10,20,15
30 PRINT "THE AVERAGE IS";(A+B+C)/3
40 END
RUN

FIG11          10:06



THE AVERAGE IS 15



Time:  0.03 secs.

Ready
SAVE FIG1.BAS

Ready
BYE
Confirm: F
Job 17, User [10101,1]  Logged off TTY10     1006
Saved all files (205 blocks)
Runtime 0.38 Sec
```

Figure 1-1

NEW command fulfills both of these functions. It can be used in two forms:

NEW <filename. extension>

e.g. **NEW PROGR.BAS**

or, simply, **NEW**

In the second case, the user is prompted to provide filename and extension, as shown in figure 1.2.

NEW
New file name -- PROGR.BAS
Ready

Figure 1-2

At this point, the program can be typed in as shown in figure 1-1.

1.4.2 Storing and Retrieving a Program

The NEW command sets up a file in core into which the user enters a program. As explained earlier, this file is not permanently stored, but will be destroyed if another file is created subsequently or if the user logs off. Several commands can be used to transfer the file to permanent storage, i.e. the disk.

If the name given to the file in core is unique, i.e., has not been used previously for a disk file, the command

SAVE

will place a copy of the program in core into a disk file with the same name. The original remains in core. The file name will be entered into a directory of files in the user area so that the file can later be retrieved.

If another file with the same name is already stored on disk, the SAVE command will elicit an error message, as shown in figure 1-3. At this point, the user has two options.

```
Ready
SAVE

? Duplicate file name -- REPLACE or RENAME
Ready
```

Figure 1-3

The file on disk can be replaced by the file in core, using the command

REPLACE

This is frequently done when the program in core is an updated version of that on disk.

It is also possible to use an extended form of the SAVE command:

SAVE <filename.extension>

and specify a new filename; in this case, the file in core will be copied to the disk file specified in the SAVE command.

If, at a later time, the disk file is needed in core (for example, for execution in a later session at the terminal), it can be loaded into core with the command

OLD <filename. extension>

e.g. **OLD PROGR.BAS**

If the filename is not specified, the user will be prompted to provide it, as shown in figure 1-4.

```
OLD
Old file name -- PROGR.BAS
READY
```

Figure 1-4

1.4.3 Program Execution

The program that has been created in core following the NEW command or that has been loaded using the OLD command has to be compiled (translated into machine language) and executed to provide the desired results to the user. The command to accomplish compilation and execution is

RUN

Following a RUN command, certain error messages may be printed (see section 1-5), or the program will be executed. Figure 1-1 illustrates the results of the RUN command.

1.4.4 Listing the Program

It may be desirable for a variety of reasons to list a program once it has been typed in or copied from disk to core: for example, changes may have been made, or the user may not remember which program is stored under a given file-name. The command

LIST

or **LIST** n_1 - n_2

can be used to type out an entire program or all statements between n_1 and n_2 inclusive.

1.4.5 Logging Off

After all the user's programs have been executed satisfactorily, it is time to log off. This is necessary for bookkeeping purposes; if a user simply walks away from the terminal, the system keeps his job alive for some time and has to supervise more jobs than are actually active. To leave the terminal, the user types

BYE

Figure 1-1 shows an example of the ensuing interaction.

1.5 Debugging the Program

Although we all strive to be perfect, it does happen at times that a program is typed in that has mistakes in it. These can be of several types: 1) syntactical errors, 2) logical errors, 3) data errors. Before a program is used on large quantities of important data, it has to be tested with data for which the results can easily be checked, and debugged, i.e., the errors removed.

Syntactical errors occur when a statement is not typed in according to the rules of BASIC. The compiler will check each statement as it is typed in and will give an error message if syntactical errors are detected. In figure 1-5, the word READ is mistyped in statement 10; an error message appears immediately. This error can be corrected by retyping statement 10 correctly, as was done in the example.

```
NEW FIG16.BAS

Ready
10 REDA X,Y,Z
? Illegal statement keyword
10 READ X,Y,Z
20 DATA 10,20,15
30 LET A = X+Y+Z/3
40 PRINT "THE AVERAGE IS" A
50 GO TO 100
60 END
RUN
```

```
FIG16          10:08


? Undefined line number 100 in line 50


Time:  0.03 secs.

Ready
50 GO TO 10
RUN

FIG16          10:09



THE AVERAGE IS 35

? Out of DATA in line 10


Time:  0.04 secs.

Ready
30 LET A = (X+Y+Z)/3
RUN

FIG16          10:09



THE AVERAGE IS 15

? Out of DATA in line 10


Time:  0.04 secs.
```

Figure 1-5

Statement 50 refers to statement 100 which does not exist. This error cannot be detected while the program is typed in; it is detected when the program is prepared for execution following the RUN statement. At this time, an error message is given (see figure 1-5) and execution stops.

To correct this error, simply retype the statement correctly. Since the program is still in core, the incorrect statement will simply be replaced by the new statement.

After this latest correction, the program will run, i.e., it will produce output. However, a quick check will show that the average of 10, 20, and 15 is 15 and not 35. This error cannot be detected by the computer since only the user knows what he intended the program to do. Therefore, he has to run the program with test data and see if it produces the desired results; if not, he needs to go back and make another correction as shown in figure 1-5.

The remaining error message, OUT OF DATA IN LINE 10, may not indicate any error if it was intended to execute statements 10 through 40 only once. Details on the READ statement, the OUT OF DATA message, and program termination will be deferred to later chapters.

EXERCISES

1. Briefly describe the following terms:
   BASIC
   CORE
   DISK
   PROGRAM
   FILE

2. Briefly describe the functions of the following commands:
   LOGIN
   R BASIC
   NEW
   OLD
   SAVE
   REPLACE
   LIST
   RUN
   BYE

3. Write a complete procedure (all necessary statements) for a given program such as:

```
10  PRINT "TESTING PROCEDURE"
20  END
```

a. Entering the program and saving it for future use.
b. Obtaining a previously saved program.
c. Modify a saved program, then replacing it with a new version. Assume that the modification is adding a line as:

   5 PRINT "BASIC PROGRAMMING"

d. Requesting a listing of the modified program.

2

Terms and Simple Statements

2.1 Introduction

For the beginner, a computer program may seem very difficult to write and understand. Yet for those who are familiar with a programming language, it becomes an enjoyable challenge to create a program that does exactly what is needed and does it with as little cost as possible. Since computers do not think but precisely follow instructions, the programmer has to solve problems in a logical and structured way and has to communicate each step in the procedure clearly to the computer. A computer program is composed of step-by-step instructions leading from the input of data to the printed output of results.

To write programs in BASIC, one has to become familiar with the building blocks of the BASIC language. In this chapter, we will introduce simple statements (or instructions for the computer). Using only these statements, one may write and execute a complete program.

To illustrate these statements, let us look at a program which solves a simple problem: to compute the average of three numbers. Figure 1-1 already introduced such a program, but let us look at it again in figure 2-1.

A program consists of a series of statements. Each statement contains a statement number, a keyword, and the statement content, as illustrated below:

10	READ	A, B, C
Statement Number – n	Keyword	Content

```
10 READ A,B,C
20 DATA 10,20,15
30 PRINT "THE AVERAGE IS";(A+B+C)/3
40 END
RUN

FIG11           10:06


THE AVERAGE IS 15
```

Figure 2-1

The statement content is usually one or more of the following: constants, variables, arithmetic or logical operators, literals, and delimiters. In the following sections, we will discuss the building blocks of the statements in figure 2-1 in some detail.

2.2 Constants

A combination of digits, letters, and possibly other characters that is fixed throughout the execution of the program is called a constant. BASIC allows two kinds of constants, numeric and string constants.

2.2.1 Numeric Constants

A numeric constant is a positive or negative integer or a number expressed in decimal or scientific notation; examples are 25, −1.25, or 2.0E−1.

Only a limited number of places are set aside internally to store a numeric constant. The maximum number of significant digits varies from one computer to another. The DEC10, for example, provides for seven digits. Thus, the constant 1234567 is stored as it is; a constant with more than seven digits, such as 123456789, is stored in exponential (scientific) notation as 1.23457E+08.

Figure 2-2 shows some numeric constants and the value that is stored internally. Note that the sign does not occupy one of the seven available positions, but a decimal point does, as is illustrated by the last line of figure 2-2.

Constant	Value Stored
1234567	1234567
123456789	1.23457 E + 8
−1234567	−1234567
123456.7	123457.

Figure 2-2

When a constant is too large (such as 12345678, overflow) or too small (such as 0.000000012, underflow) so that more than seven digits are needed, it is stored in scientific notation. A number in scientific notation consists of two parts, the mantissa and the exponent, as shown below:

$$\underbrace{1.23457}_{\text{mantissa}}\ \underbrace{E + 8}_{\text{exponent}}$$

The exponent contains the letter E and a two-digit number by which the mantissa should be multiplied. Using scientific notation, constants on the DEC10 can vary in magnitude between 10^{-38} and 1.7×10^{38}.

To convert from scientific to decimal notation, one simply multiplies the mantissa by the appropriate power of 10, or shifts the decimal point as many places as the exponent indicates. Figure 2-3 illustrates the conversion.

2.2.2 String Constants

Any non-numeric constant (containing letters, special characters, or even a group of digits) is called a string constant. A string constant is a group of characters enclosed by quotes; "USA 81" is an example. A string constant may contain any character (symbol) normally used in

Scientific Notation	Decimal Equivalent
1.25 E + 4	12500
1.25 E + 3	1250
1.25 E + 2	125
1.25 E + 1	12.5
1.25 E + 0	1.25
1.25 E − 1	0.125
1.25 E − 2	0.0125
1.25 E − 3	0.00125
1.25 E − 4	0.000125

Figure 2-3

BASIC: letters, digits, punctuation symbols, and special characters such as "+" or "$"

Note: a number enclosed in quotes, such as "6", is a string constant and cannot be used interchangeably with a numeric constant such as 6. All of the combinations in figure 2-4 are acceptable string constants.

"UNITED STATES"
"376-11-1234"
"AB3*?2"
"WHAT ?"

Figure 2-4

2.3 Variables

A variable can assume several values throughout execution of the program. One can think of a variable name as a label attached to a specific location in memory; different constants can be stored in succession in that location during program execution. For example, in the statement

10 READ A,B,C

the letters A, B, and C are the names of three numeric variables. As will be explained in section 2.4, the READ statement will cause numeric values to be stored in these three locations.

Although different values can be stored in a location, they all have to be of the same type, i.e., numeric or string constants. For example, two memory locations may have labels and contents as follow

MAY	1981
M$	Y

The memory location M$ contains the string constant MAY and the memory location Y contains the numeric constant 1981. M$ is referred to as a string variable and Y as a numeric variable.

Every time a new variable name is encountered in the program, a memory location is set aside and labelled with that variable name. During program execution, different values can be stored in these locations either with the READ statement (section 2.4) or with the assignment statement (chapter 3).

Figure 2-5 shows a brief overview of the types of variables that can be encountered in BASIC. Only simple variables will be discussed in the next few chapters; subscripted variables will be treated in Chapter 6.

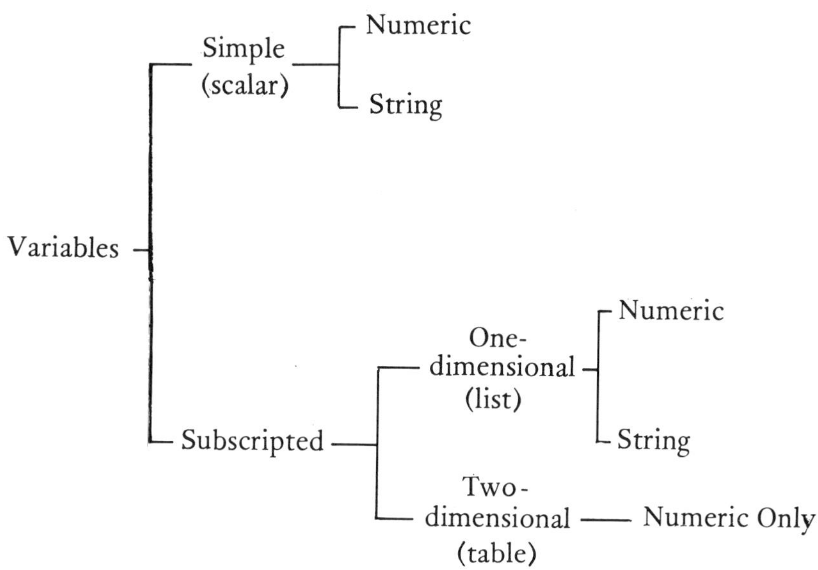

Fig. 2-5

Whether a location is to be used for numeric or string values is indicated by the variable name. The rules for the assignment of variable names follow.

2.3.1 Numeric Variable Names

A numeric variable name can have one of two forms:

1. A single letter of the alphabet, such as A or Z; or
2. A single letter followed by a single digit, such as A1 or Z9.

Figure 2-6 shows valid and invalid names for numeric variables.

Name	Valid?	Reason
A	Yes	Single letter
5	No	Not a letter
B3	Yes	Letter + single digit
AI	No	Two letters not acceptable
9C	No	Letter must come first
D12	No	Too many digits

Figure 2-6

2.3.2 String Variable Names

String variables are identified by a $ sign; they can have one of two forms:

1. Single letter followed by a $ sign, such as A$, S$;
   or
2. Single letter followed by a single digit and followed by a $ sign, such as A1$; B9$. Figure 2-7 shows some valid and invalid string variable names.

Name	Valid?	Reason
B$	Yes	Form (1)
6C$	No	Letter must come first
B1$	Yes	Form (2)
XY$	No	Second character must be a digit
$D2	No	Name must end with a $, not start with it

Figure 2-7

2.4 READ and DATA Statements

We have discussed constants and variables as building blocks of BASIC statements. We are now ready to introduce the first set of statements.

These two statements are used to assign values to variables. Their general form is:

n READ <variable list>

and

n DATA <list of constants>.

where n is the statement number, the variable list contains one or more variable names (both numeric and string variables are legal), and the list of constants contains numeric and/or string constants.

During program execution, the first constant in a DATA statement is assigned to the first variable in a READ statement, the second constant is stored in the second variable, etc. This is illustrated in figure 2-8.

```
10  READ    X,    Y,       A$
            ↕     ↕        ↕
20  DATA   10,   20,  "MARCH"
```

Figure 2-8

The following rules apply for these two statements:

1. Each program that contains a READ statement must contain at least one DATA statement.
2. There should be at least as many constants listed on DATA statements as there are variable names on READ statements. If not, execution of the program will stop, and a message "OUT OF DATA IN LINE n" will be printed.
3. Variable names and corresponding constants must be of the same type. An attempt to read a numeric value into a string variable or a string value into a numeric variable may result in an error message.
4. The DATA statements can be placed anywhere in the program as long as they precede the END statement. Data can be placed on one or more DATA statements. During execution time all the DATA statements will be treated as equivalent to one list of constants, these constants will be arranged in the same order as they appear in the program, and values will be taken from the list as READ statements are encountered.

Figure 2-9 shows several short programs, all designed to read the same set of data. The PRINT statement is used to show how the data were read; this statement will be explained in the next section.

```
FIG28B          11:47

10 READ X,Y
20 READ A$,B$
30 DATA 10,20
40 PRINT X,Y,A$,B$
50 DATA "HAMMER"
60 DATA "NAIL"
70 END

Ready
RUN

FIG28B          11:47


10              20              HAMMER          NAIL



FIG28A          11:46


10 DATA 10,20,"HAMMER","NAIL"
20 READ X,Y,A$,B$
30 PRINT X,Y,A$,B$
40 END

Ready
RUNNH

10              20              HAMMER          NAIL



FIG28C          11:48



10 READ X,Y,A$,B$
20 DATA 10,"NAIL",20,"HAMMER"
30 PRINT X,Y,A$,B$
40 END

Ready
RUNNH


10              20              NAIL            HAMMER
```

```
FIG29D          11:48



10 READ X,Y,A$,B$
20 DATA 10,20,"HAMMER"
30 PRINT X,Y,A$,B$
40 END

Ready
RUNNH



? Out of DATA in line 10
```

Figure 2-9

Programs FIG28A and FIG28B both accomplish the same goal. They illustrate that it does not matter how many READ and DATA statements are used as long as the total number of variable names does not exceed the total number of constants. The placement of the DATA statements is also immaterial.

Programs FIG28C and FIG28D illustrate two errors that are frequently made when using READ and DATA statements. Constants in the DATA statements should be in the same order as the corresponding variables; however, in some systems the computer will seek out the next numeric constant to match the numeric variable X, and will skip the *next* constant, "NAIL", until it is requested. If insufficient data are provided, program execution will stop.

2.5 The PRINT Statement

In a way, the most important statements in a program are output statements, and the PRINT statement is a good example. One can imagine a computer program that runs for 30 minutes doing some very complex computations and then stops without printing. The program may have performed satisfactorily, but if the results are not communicated, the user is no wiser at the end. The results that are stored in memory will be lost and can only be retrieved by running the program again. Thus, every program has at least one output statement to communicate the results, and the PRINT statement is commonly used for that purpose.

2.5.1 PRINT Statement

The general form of the PRINT statement is:

n PRINT < list >

where n is the statement number and list may contain variables, constants, expressions, or literals, or it may be empty. Some common uses of the PRINT statement are:

1. Print the values of variables, constants, or expressions. An example is:

   ```
   10 PRINT    R,        3.14,       3.14 * R * R
            variable   constant     expression
   ```

   Arithmetic expressions are discussed in detail in chapter 3.

2. Print text (literals). An example is:

   20 PRINT "COMPUTATION BEGINS"

   The entire string of 18 characters, including the space, is printed. Literals have to be enclosed in quotation marks.

3. Print a blank line. The only available means for providing vertical spacing in BASIC is the PRINT statement. A statement such as

   30 PRINT

   causes a blank line to be printed.

Figure 2-10 shows a sample program with several PRINT statements. Study the output carefully to see what the statements do. You will see both string and numeric values printed out. Note also that the variable names A, B, C are used twice and, thus, change value as a new READ statement is encountered.

You may have noticed that the elements of the output list are separated by semicolons and commas. These delimiters perform a specific function in the PRINT statement.

2.5.2 Use of Commas

A comma in a PRINT statement causes the information to be printed in a full print zone format. The exact length of the print zone varies slightly from one system to the next. On the DEC10, the available print space (72 characters) is divided into five zones and each is 14 characters in length. When commas are used to separate items in the output list, each item is printed in a separate print zone, as illustrated in figure 2-11.

```
FIG29           11:49


 10 PRINT "THIS PROGRAM PRINTS AVERAGES"
 20 PRINT
 30 PRINT "  A ";"  B ";"  C ";"AVERAGE"
 40 PRINT
 50 DATA 10,20,30,45,60,75
 60 READ A,B,C
 70 PRINT A;B;C;(A+B+C)/3
 75 PRINT
 80 READ A,B,C
 85 PRINT " A"," B"," C","AVERAGE"
 90 PRINT A,B,C,(A+B+C)/3
 100 END

Ready
RUN

FIG29           11:49


THIS PROGRAM PRINTS AVERAGES

  A   B   C AVERAGE

 10  20  30  20

 A             B             C             AVERAGE
 45            60            75             60
```

Figure 2-10

Each "-" indicates one print position. Note that numeric values are printed with a sign position (blank if positive) and left justified. As was shown in section 2.2, a numeric value can occupy at most 12 print positions (sign, seven digit number, 4 character exponent) and fits always into a print zone.

12	0.05	245

Figure 2-11

Printing string values may cause a problem since they are not restricted in length. If a string value occupies more than 14 characters, it will be printed in two zones, and the next item will then be printed in the third print zone. This might cause problems with headings, as is illustrated in figure 2-12.

Figure 2-12

There are two ways to remedy this situation: restrict the first heading to one print zone, or have the second value printed into the third print zone. These are illustrated in the program in figure 2-13. In statement 40 two consecutive commas are used to assign C to the third print zone. This works because each comma causes the carriage to move to the next print zone.

```
10 A=12
20 B=.05
30 C=245
35 PRINT "AMOUNT","MONTHLY BONUS RATE","COMM."
40 PRINT A,B,,C
50 END

Ready
RUN

PRINT.2          11:22


AMOUNT           MONTHLY BONUS RATE             COMM.
 12               0.05                           245
```

Figure 2-13

Obviously only five values can be printed on one line, using commas as delimiters. If more than five items are listed in the PRINT statements, the sixth and following values will automatically be printed in the next line. Figure 2-14 illustrates this point.

```
10 REM ILLUSTRATION OF USING COMMAS IN THE PRINT STATEMENT
20 PRINT "THE TEMPERATURES OF THE WEEK"
25 PRINT
30 PRINT "MON","TUES","WED","THURS","FRI","SAT","SUN"
40 READ D1,D2,D3,D4,D5,D6,D7
50 PRINT D1,D2,D3,D4,D5,D6,D7
60 DATA 28,30,35,42,36,32,25
70 END

Ready
RUN

PRINT.COM      11:23


THE TEMPERATURES OF THE WEEK

MON           TUES          WED           THURS         FRI
SAT           SUN
 28            30            35            42            36
 32            25
```

Figure 2-14

2.5.3 Use of Semicolons

Frequently all the values to be printed are small so that 14 print positions per zone are more than are needed; on the other hand, one may want to print more than five values on a line. This can be done by using a semicolon as a delimiter instead of a comma.

If two items in the PRINT statement are separated by a semicolon, they will be printed adjacent to each other. For string items, a semicolon implies that they will be printed without separating blanks. Numeric items are always printed with a sign position and a trailing blank. Thus, they are separated by one or two blanks as shown in figure 2-15.

A variation of the program to print the temperatures of the week is shown in figure 2-16. Since each two-digit number occupies four print positions, the names of the days have been abbreviated to no more than three characters, which makes it possible to align titles and values.

```
10 PRINT "POWERS"; "OF"; "-2"
20 PRINT -2; 4; -8; 16; -32
30 END

Ready
RUN

TEST.ABC        11:27



POWERSOF-2
-2  4 -8  16 -32
```

Figure 2-15

```
10 REM ILLUSTRATION OF USING SEMICOLON IN THE PRINT STATEMENT
20 PRINT "THE TEMPERATURES OF THE WEEK"
25 PRINT
30 PRINT "MON ";" TU ";" WED";" TH ";" FRI";" SAT";" SUN"
40 READ D1,D2,D3,D4,D5,D6,D7
50 PRINT D1;D2;D3;D4;D5;D6;D7
60 DATA 28,30,35,42,36,32,25
70 END

Ready
RUN

PRINT.SEM      11:28



THE TEMPERATURES OF THE WEEK

MON  TU  WED TH  FRI SAT SUN
 28  30  35  42  36  32  25
```

Figure 2-16

Other methods to arrange printout on the line are discussed in chapter 7.

2.6 STOP and END Statements

You have no doubt noticed that all sample programs contain a statement that we have not yet discussed: the END statement.

Every BASIC program must have an END statement. Its form is very simple

n END

where n is the highest statement number in the program since the END statement must be the last statement in the program. Statements following the END would not be compiled or executed.

Some computer systems also accept the statement

n STOP

for terminating the execution of the program. There can be more than one STOP statement, and STOP statements can be located anywhere in the program. But even if a STOP statement is used, it is still necessary to end the program with an END statement. In general, a STOP statement is not necessary.

2.7 REM Statement

Another statement that is useful at times is the REM statement. This is non-executable; the computer simply ignores it at execution time.

The REM statement allows the programmer to put comments into the program. This may make it easier to understand the program at a later time. The general form of the REM statement is

n REM <text>

where n is the statement number and text can be anything the programmer wants to write.

Figure 2-16 shows all the statements discussed in this chapter. At this point, the reader should be able to write simple programs, such as that shown in figure 2-16, which are input/output oriented. In chapter 3 computational statements will be introduced.

EXERCISES

1. Define the terms "constant" and "variable". Give two examples each for the types of constants.
2. Define the function of each of the statements introduced in this chapter, such as:
   READ
   DATA
   PRINT

3. Write each of the following numbers in decimal form:
   a. 1.3456E+03
   b. 123.56E+05
   c. 0.1345E−02
   d. 1.3450E−02
   e. 12345E−04
4. Identify and correct the errors in the following numeric constants (some may be correct).
   a. 3.5^2
   b. 2,560,000.00
   c. 2,64E+03
   d. 1.2345E125
   e. 236.80E1.2
   f. 2 1/2
   g. 374−42−1245
   h. "12456"
   i. 0.00256E3
   j. 0.00256E−4
5. Identify and correct the errors in the following string constants (some may be correct).
   a. **A2**
   b. **"125"**
   c. **"MS220-1"**
   d. **12E4**
   e. **"A NICE DAY"**
   f. **16-MAY-81**
6. Identify the following BASIC variable names as unacceptable, numeric, or string.
   a. **G$2**
   b. **AB**
   c. **AZ$**
   d. **C1B**
   e. **BS**
   f. **$A**
   g. **2B**
   h. **A14**
   i. **ABC**
   j. **X**

7. Give the value each variable would have after the following program segments are executed.

a.
```
40 READ A,B,C
50 READ D,E
60 DATA 25,31,20,40,36
```

b.
```
40 READ A
50 DATA 2,3,4,2,5,7
60 READ B
70 READ D,F,C,E
```

c.
```
40 READ D$,M$,Y$
50 DATA "26","MAY","81"
```

d.
```
40 READ Y$,M$,D$
50 DATA "26","MAY"
60 DATA "81"
```

8. Write the READ and DATA statements to assign values as described:
   a. Sea level pressure is 30 inches, barometer indication is 9.4 inches, and altitude in feet is 29012.19.
   b. The day is 30, the month is April, and the year is 1981.
   c. The starting point is Muncie, the destination is Indianapolis, and the distance is 110 miles.
   d. Location of the earthquake is San Francisco, the magnitude on the Richter Scale is 7.75, and the multiplier when compared with the Nicaragua quake is 100 times.
9. Write a PRINT statement to print the information described in 8a.
10. Write a PRINT statement to print the date described in 8b in the order month, day, and year.
11. Write the PRINT statements to print the information described in 8d with each item in a separate line and double space between the first and second line of print.
12. Print the seven days of the week in one line with two spaces in between.
13. Write a program to print the letter "H" as:

```
H  H
H  H
HHHH
H  H
H  H
```

14. Identify and correct the errors that occur in some of the statements.

a.
```
10 READ A,B,C
20 DATA 20,30
```

b.
```
10 READ N$, H,3.5
20 DATA "SMITH",30
```

c.
```
10 READ C$,S$,Z$
20 DATA "MUNCIE","INDIANA",47305
```

d.
```
30 PRINT CITY,STATE,ZIP
```

e.
```
30 PRINT "DISTANCE" "SPEED"
```

f.
```
30 PRINT "TIME 15";D/S;"MINUTES"
```

g.
```
30 PRINT "DISTANCE"=,D
```

h.
```
30 PRINT
```

i.
```
40 READ A=3.5,B=2,6
```

Programming Problems

1. Write a program that reads the coefficients (a,b,c) of a polynomial and prints out the polynomial in algebraic form as:

   $ax^2 + bx + c$

   Let a = 21, b = -16, and c = -2

2. Results from a physics experiment are:

   a. Weight of an object in the atmosphere = 125.2

   b. Weight of the same object suspended underwater = 112.4

   c. Weight of displaced water = 125.2 / 12.8 = 9.78125

   Prepare a program to read the above information and print the information described with the title "Specific gravity determination."

3. Write a program that prints the word "ENGINE". The first two letters should appear as shown.

```
EEEEE   N     N
E       NN    N
EEEEE   N  N  N
E       N    NN
EEEEE   N     N
```

You may design the remaining letters yourself.

3

Computations in BASIC

3.1 Introduction

In the preceding chapter we discussed how constants and variables are stored in the computer and how they can be read in and printed out. Although it is important to be able to read and print, this is not the main thrust of engineering applications of the computer. Typically the computer is used to perform a large number of computations which may produce a printout of only one number in some cases.

Computations in BASIC can range from performing simple algebraic operations such as $y = ax^2 + bx + c$ to finding the roots of transcendental functions or solving systems of linear equations. Any computation that is needed can be programmed in BASIC; many functions that are commonly used are available, and the user can program additional functions where necessary.

The basic arithmetic operations and built-in functions will be discussed in this chapter. Matrix operations, iterative methods, and user-defined functions will be handled in later chapters.

3.2 Basic Arithmetic Operations

Constants and variables are combined with arithmetic operators to form arithmetic expressions. Examples of arithmetic expressions are A * B, A + B/2, and C − D * * 3. Figure 3-1 shows the arithmetic operators used in BASIC.

Operation	Operator in BASIC	Example
Addition	+	**A + B**
Subtraction	−	**A − B**
Multiplication	*	**A * B**
Division	/	**A/B**
Exponentiation	* * or ↑	**A * * B or A ↑ B**
Sign reversal	−	**−A**

Figure 3-1

The arithmetic operators are never implied. We might write 3x in a formula, but 3x would not be a valid arithmetic expression in BASIC: it has to be written 3 * X.

If several variables are combined in one arithmetic expression, rules of precedence apply. According to these rules (see figure 3-2), multiplication and division are performed before addition. Therefore, 3*4 + 5/10 = 12 + .5 = 12.5

Level	Operators
1	↑, ** (Exponentiation)
2	— (Sign reversal)
3	* / (Multiplication, Division)
4	+ — (Addition, Subtraction)

Figure 3-2

All operations on level 1 are performed before any operations on levels 2, 3, or 4 are performed; level 2 operations take precedence over level 3 and 4 operations; and level 3 operations are executed before level 4 operations. Operations on the same level are executed from left to right. It is important that the programmer be aware of this hierarchy so that statements can be written correctly.

If a deviation from the order shown in figure 3-2 is desired, parentheses can be used. Expressions in parentheses are evaluated first — and according to the rules in figure 3-2. The following examples illustrate arithmetic expressions and their evaluation.

Example 1: Which of the following arithmetic expressions correctly represents

$$\frac{a + b/c}{d + e/f}?$$

1. A + B/C/D + E/F
2. A + B/C/(D + E/F)
3. (A + B/C) / D + E/F
4. (A + B/C) / (D + E/F)

Let us discuss them one at a time. In (1), the highest level operations are divisions, and these are performed from left to right. Thus, C will be divided into B and then D will be divided into the result. Also, F will be divided into E. The two results (B/C/D and E/F) will then be added to A.

In (2), the expression in parentheses will be evaluated first. Within the parentheses, the division will be performed first. Thus, F will be divided into E and the result added to D. After this, divisions will be performed from left to right; C will be divided into B, the value computed earlier (D + E/F) will be divided into B/C, and the result will be added to A.

In (3), C will be divided into B, the result added to A, and the resulting value divided by D. Then E will be divided by F and the result added to the value obtained earlier.

Finally in (4), both parentheses will be evaluated. C will be divided into B and the result added to A. F will be divided into E and the result added to D. Then the numerator result will be divided by the denominator. This is the correct BASIC expression for the fraction given.

Figure 3-3 shows the results of the four expressions for A = 10, B = 12, C = 2, D = 2, E = 18, and F = 3. The reader should check to make sure he/she can arrive at the same solutions.

Expression	Value
A + B/C/D + E/F	10 + 12/2/2 + 18/3 = 19
A + B/C/(D + E/F)	10 + 12/2/(2 + 18/3) = 10.75
(A + B/C)/D + E/F	(10 + 12/2)/2 + 18/3 = 14
(A + B/C)/(D + E/F)	(10 + 12/2)/(2 + 18/3) = 2

Figure 3-3

Example 2: What is the value of −2 * * 4/8?
As was indicated in Figure 3-2, exponentiation is the first operation to

be performed. Thus, 2 * * 4 is the first step in the evaluation of this expression; next, the sign is reversed; and, finally, the division is performed. Thus,

$$-2 ** 4/8 = -2^4/8 = -16/8 = -2$$

If the intent was $(-2)^4/8$, then parentheses would have been used, the expression in BASIC would be (−2) * * 4/8 and the value would be +2.

3.3 The LET Statement

After computations have been performed, the result has to be stored under a variable name so that it can be referenced later in the program, for example in a PRINT statement. This is done with the assignment or LET statement. This statement has the general form

n LET[1] <variable> = ⟨constant, variable, expression, or function⟩

where n is the statement number, variable is the name of the location where the result is to be stored, and the value to the right of the equal sign (=) is the value to be stored. If an expression or function is on the right side of the equal sign (=), it will be evaluated before the assignment takes place. Examples for LET statements are

```
10 LET A = 0
20 LET B = A
30 LET C = (A + B) * * 2
```

So far we have discussed the LET statement only for numerical variables. It can also be used for string variables. Thus,

```
40 LET D$ ="GOOD"
```

is a valid LET statement. Note that the type of the variable on the left of the = sign (receiving variable) has to be the same as that of the constant, variable, or expression on the right. Thus,

```
50 LET A= B$
```

or

```
60 LET B$ =10
```

---

[1] The word LET is optional

is invalid; a string variable cannot be assigned to a numerical variable or vice versa.

The equal sign is an assignment operator and not a relational operator. This means that

70 LET N = N + 1

is a legitimate statement; the expression on the right will be evaluated and the result will be stored in the location assigned to the variable N. Also, since the LET is an assignment statement, it is not possible to write a statement such as

80 LET N + 1 = N

Statement 80 would imply that the value of N is to be stored in the location N + 1. But N + 1 is not a legal variable name; thus, an error message results.

If, at the beginning of a program, several variables should be set to the same initial value, a multiple LET can be used. This has the form

n LET var1 = var2 = . . . = varn = ⟨constant, variable or expression⟩

where var1, var2, . . ., varn are the names of the variables to be initialized. For example,

90 LET A = B = C = 0

will set the variables A, B, and C to 0.

A simple program illustrating the LET statement is shown in figure 3-4. Statement 30 is a multiple LET statement; the printout from statement 70 shows that all 3 variables are indeed equal to 50. Statement 40 through 60 show the computation of (A + B/C)/(D + E/F), $-A^3 + B*E/D$, and $\sqrt{B^2 + C^2}$, respectively. The results are shown in the printout.

3.4 Built-in Functions

Statement 60 in figure 3-4 illustrated one way to find a square root. Square root is one of the functions frequently used in engineering applications, for example to compute the distance between two points. Other functions are also needed — logarithms, the exponential function, trigonometric functions.

All these functions are available in BASIC. Table 3-1 shows a list of all the built-in functions available on the DEC10.

```
10 READ A,B,C,D,E,F
20 DATA 10,20,30,7,14,21
30 LET S1=S2=S3=50
40 LET X=(A+B/C)/(D+E/F)
50 LET Y = -A**3 + B*E/D
60 LET Z=(B**2 + C**2)**.5
70 PRINT S1,S2,S3
80 PRINT A,B,C
90 PRINT D,E,F
100 PRINT X,Y,Z
110 END

Ready
RUN

FIG34           10:21

50              50              50
10              20              30
7               14              21
1.3913         -960             36.0555
```

Figure 3-4

Function	BASIC Name
Sine of X	**SIN(X)**
Cosine of X	**COS(X)**
Tangent of X	**TAN(X)**
Cotangent of X	**COT(X)**
Arctangent of X	**ATN(X)**
Exponential function	**EXP(X)**
Natural logarithm (base e)	**LOG(X), LN(X), LOGE(X)**
Common logarithm (base 10)	**CLOG(X), LOG10(X)**
Square root	**SQR(X)**
Absolute value	**ABS(X)**
Greatest integer $\leq$ X	**INT(X)**
Sign function 1 for X >0 0 for X $=0$ -1 for x <0	**SGN(X)**
Random number between 0 and 1	**RND**

Table 3-1
Built-in Functions in BASIC

The built-in functions can be used as parts of an arithmetic expression or alone on the right side of a LET statement. For example, statement 60 in figure 3-4 could be rewritten as

```
60 LET Z = SQR (B * * 2 + C * * 2)
```

The argument of a built-in function can be a numeric constant, a numeric variable, or an arithmetic expression.

Most of these functions should be familiar to the reader. The RND function does not require an argument and will return a random value between 0 and 1. If a random integer between A and B is desired, this can be obtained through the statement

```
100 LET Y = INT((B - A) * RND + A)
```

For example,

```
110 LET Y = INT (99 * RND + 1)
```

would produce a random number between 1 and 100. If RND =.5, for example [1]

$$Y = [99 * .5 + 1] = [50.5] = 50$$

If a trigonometric function is needed for an angle measured in degrees, this angle has to be converted to radian before it can be used as argument for the function in BASIC. For example, to find sin (90°) in BASIC, one needs the statements

```
200 LET X = 90/360 *2* 3.1415
210 LET Y = SIN(X)
```

or, simply

```
250 LET Y = SIN (90/360 * 2 * 3.1415)
```

Some examples of programs using arithmetic expressions and built-in functions are given in the next section.

3.5 Examples

At this point, it is difficult to provide meaningful examples since transfer of control statements have not yet been discussed and each statement is, therefore, executed only once. Figures 3-5, 3-7, 3-8 and

---

[1] $[x]$ = greatest integer $\leqslant X$

3-9 show sample programs to solve equations or compute values for selected formulas. These sample programs could, at a later time, be incorporated into programs performing a series of computations. The exercises at the end of this chapter provide further opportunity to practice the use of LET statements and functions.

Example 1: Solving a quadratic equation.

An equation of the form $ax^2 + bx + c = 0$ is called a quadratic equation. Its roots are given by the formula

$$x_{1,2} = \frac{-b \pm \sqrt{b^2 - 4ac}}{2a}$$

This formula gives both real and complex roots. However, the square root function in BASIC will accept only non-negative arguments. Thus, only real roots can be found using BASIC. Figure 3-5 shows a program to find the roots of a quadratic equation for 3 cases — 2 roots, 1 root, and no real roots.

For the equation $x^2 + 10x + 30$, $b^2 - 4ac = 100 - 120 < 0$. This leads to an error message when the SQR function is called (see figure 3-5). The program then ignores the minus sign and proceeds; the roots given are computed by using $\sqrt{20}$ instead of $\sqrt{-20}$.

This is, of course, an unsatisfactory result. The programmer should test if $b^2 - 4ac < 0$ and, if so, not compute the roots and write out an appropriate message. How to do this is discussed in chapter 4.

Example 2: The use of trigonometric functions can be illustrated in a program to compute the distance travelled and total flight time for a particle.[1] Figure 3-6 shows the variables of interest.

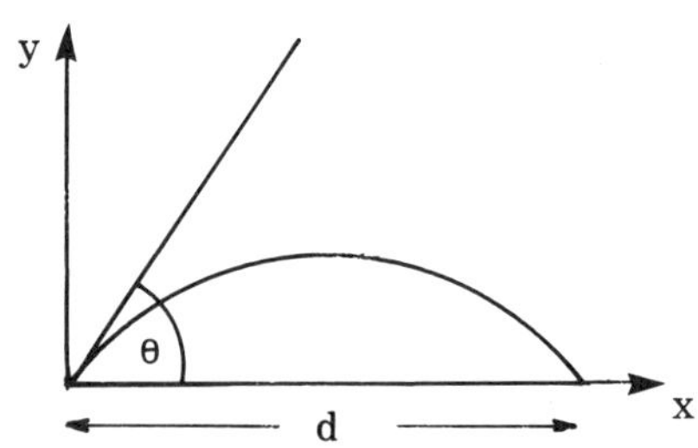

Figure 3-6

[1] Formulas in this example are taken from Mott Sounders, *The Engineer's Companion*, New York: John Wiley and Sons, Inc.

```
10 DATA 1,2,-35,2,-100,1250,1,10,30
20 READ A1,B1,C1,A2,B2,C2,A3,B3,C3
30 LET T = SQR(B1**2 - 4*A1*C1)
40 LET X1=(-B1+T)/(2*A1)
50 LET X2=(-B1-T)/(2*A1)
60 PRINT "A =" A1,"B ="B1,"C ="C1
70 PRINT "X1 =" X1, "X2 =" X2
80 LET T = SQR(B2**2 - 4*A2*C2)
90 LET X1 = (-B2+T)/(2*A2)
100 LET X2 = (-B2-T)/(2*A2)
110 PRINT "A =" A2, "B =" B2, "C =" C2
120 PRINT "X1 =" X1, "X2 ="X2
130 LET T = SQR(B3**2 - 4*A3*C3)
140 LET X1 = (-B3+T)/(2*A3)
150 LET X2 = (-B3 - T)/(2*A3)
160 PRINT "A =" A3, "B ="B3, "C =" C3
170 PRINT "X1 =" X1, "X2 =" X2
180 END

Ready
RUN

FIG35           10:22



A = 1           B = 2           C =-35
X1 = 5          X2 =-7
A = 2           B =-100         C = 1250
X1 = 25         X2 = 25

% SQRT of negative number in line 130
A = 1           B = 10          C = 30
X1 =-2.76393    X2 =-7.23607
```

Figure 3-5

It can be shown that a particle leaving the origin (x = 0, y = 0) at time t = 0 travels on a parabola if air resistance is neglected. If the initial velocity is V_0 and the flight path starts at an angle θ, the coordinates of the particle at time t are

$$X = (V_0 \cos \theta)\, t$$
$$Y = (V_0 \sin \theta)\, t - gt^2/2$$

The total distance travelled is

$$d = V_0^2 / g \sin 2\theta$$

and the total flight time is

$$T = 2\, V_0 / g \sin \theta\, .$$

The constant g is the downward acceleration or gravitational pull; g is approximately 32.17 feet/sec².

Figure 3-7 shows a program computing d and T. The program assumes that the angle is given in degrees; statement 40 converts degrees into radian. Since g is expressed in feet/sec², V_0 has to be expressed in the same units (feet/sec), or a scale factor has to be included. In the sample program, velocity is expressed in feet/sec. The distance travelled is measured in feet and the time travelled in seconds.

```
10 DATA 150,45
20 READ V0,A0
30 LET G = 32.17
40 LET A1 = A0*3.14159/180
50 LET D = V0**2/G*SIN(2*A1)
60 LET T = 2*V0/G*SIN(A1)
70 PRINT "INITIAL SPEED" V0
80 PRINT "ANGLE " A0
90 PRINT "DISTANCE TRAVELLED " D
100 PRINT "TIME IN FLIGHT " T
110 END

Ready
RUN

PROJE          11:24



INITIAL SPEED 150
ANGLE  45
DISTANCE TRAVELLED  699.409
TIME IN FLIGHT  6.59409
```

Figure 3-7

Example 3: The intensity of a sound is measured in terms of the energy of the sound waves passing through a unit area (1 cm^2) perpendicular to the direction of the sound per second. The relative intensity of two sounds is measured in bels $= \log_{10} \frac{P_1}{P_2}$ where P_1 and P_2 indicate power of the two sources measured in microwatts; more commonly, the unit is decibels which equal 1/10 bels.

A program to compute the relative intensity of two sources is shown in figure 3-8; it illustrates the use of the LOG10 function.

```
10 READ P1,P2
20 DATA 500,700
30 LET D1 = LOG10(P1/P2)
40 LET D2 = .1*D1
50 PRINT "POWER 1", "POWER 2"
60 PRINT P1,P2
70 PRINT "RELATIVE INTENSITY"
80 PRINT D1;"BELS OR ";D2;"DECIBELS"
90 END

Ready
RUN

FIG38          11:25



POWER 1        POWER 2
 500            700
RELATIVE INTENSITY
-0.146128 BELS OR -1.46128E-2 DECIBELS
```

Figure 3-8

Example 4: An example using the exponential function can be found in finance. To compute interest on a continuous basis, the formula is

$$A = Pe^{it}$$

where i is the annual interest rate, P is the principal, t is the time in years, and A is the amount received at the end of the tth year with continuous compounding. A program using this formula is shown in figure 3-9. The same formula can also be used to compute the present value of a sum to be received at the end of t years, by simply solving for P:

$$P = Ae^{-it}$$

Statement 50 in figure 3-9 is used to compute the present value.

```
10 REM CONTINUOUS INTEREST
20 READ I,T,P,A
30 DATA .055,10,2000,2000
40 LET A1=P*EXP(I*T)
50 LET P1 = A*EXP(-I*T)
55 PRINT "INTEREST"
60 PRINT " RATE","TIME"
70 PRINT I,T
80 PRINT
90 PRINT  P;"WILL GROW TO " A1
100 PRINT A; "HAS A PRESENT VALUE OF" P1
110 END

Ready
RUN

FIG39           11:26



INTEREST
 RATE           TIME
 0.055           10

 2000 WILL GROW TO  3466.51
 2000 HAS A PRESENT VALUE OF 1153.9
```

Figure 3-9

EXERCISES

1. Show step by step the operations performed in solving the following expressions.
   a. 6 + 8/4 + 5 * 7 **2 − 14
   b. (2+4)*5**3/(7−3)+8
   c. P * (1 + R / C) ** (C * Y)
   When P = 100, R = .12, C = 1, and Y = 2

2. Write a BASIC statement for each of the following:

   a. $y = a^b + c$

   b. $y = a^{(b+c)}$

   c. $y = x^{-4}$

   d. $y = \dfrac{c_2 a_1 - c_1 a_2}{a_1 b_2 - a_2 b_1}$

   e. $y = \dfrac{x}{z} + \dfrac{5}{3}\left(\dfrac{x^2 \times w}{r}\right) - 3r$

   f. $y = x^2 + \sqrt{1 - x^2}$

   g. $y = \sqrt{x + a} - \sqrt{x}$

   h. $y = \log(x + \sqrt{x^2 + 1})$

   i. $y = e^{x \log a}$

   j. $y = \sin A \cdot \cos B - \cos A \cdot \sin B$

   k. $y = \dfrac{m}{(1 - \frac{v^2}{c^2})^{1/2}}$

Programming Problems

1. Write a program to do long division such that the result shows both the quotient and remainder if any.
2. Write a program to convert from US dollars into pounds. (Note: use the present exchange rate.)
3. Write a program to compute two sides and the remaining angle of a triangle if you are given two angles and one side. Also find the area of the triangle. Formulas are given below.

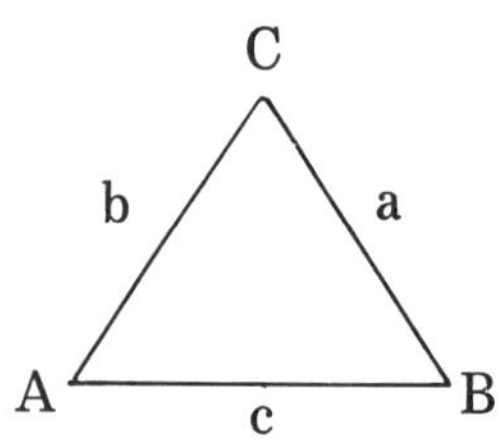

For a given a and angles A and B.

$$b = \frac{a \sin B}{\sin A}$$

$$c = \frac{a \sin C}{\sin A}$$

Area = ½ ab sin C

4. Write a program to solve any triangle with given values of two sides and the included angle.

$$C = \sqrt{a^2 + b^2 - 2ab \cos C}$$

$$A = \sin^{-1}\left(\frac{a \sin C}{c}\right)$$

Area = ½ ab sin C

5. Write a program to find the length of side c of a triangle given side b and the angle θ .

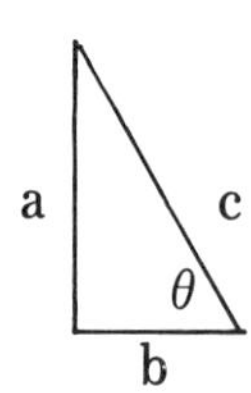

When $c = \dfrac{b}{\cos \theta}$

4

Transfer of Control — Branching

4.1 Introduction

In the last chapter statements were introduced to perform computations using both arithmetic operations and a variety of functions. The statements in the programs were executed in the order in which they were listed (ascending statement numbers), and each statement was executed only once.

However, most problems to be solved using a computer are more complex in nature. For example, in the program to solve a quadratic equation (see figure 3-5), it would be desirable to test whether $b^2 - 4ac < 0$ and then make special provisions rather than let the program compute the square root of a negative number by omitting the sign. The IF statement which will be discussed in section 4.5 allows such testing to be done in the program.

Another extension of the simple programs discussed in chapter 3 is motivated by the need to process a large number of data points. If two quadratic equations are to be solved, it is necessary to go back and execute the entire program or a part of it a second time. The GO TO statement which will be discussed in section 4.4 makes it possible to transfer control back to the beginning of the program.

As soon as a program contains decision points from which control can be tranferred to two different parts of the program (branches), there is an opportunity to make logical errors. Debugging a program with a large number of IF and GO TO statements can be quite time consuming. It becomes necessary to plan the program carefully and document the logic of the program graphically to minimize the occurrence of logical errors. A graphic representation of the program is called a flowchart. Sections 4.2 and 4.3 will introduce problem analysis and flowcharting. The transfer of control statements — GO TO and IF — will be introduced in sections 4.4 and 4.5.

4.2 Problem Analysis

Figure 4.1 outlines the entire programming process. In the beginning a problem exists that can be solved using a computer. The problem is analyzed, and the solution is diagrammed in a flowchart. From the flowchart a programmer will do the coding. In the context of this book, the coding will be done in BASIC, but the process would be identical if another programming language were used. The program is entered into the computer, debugged, and executed with test data. At this point, it may be necessary to return to earlier steps — change the coding, update the flowchart, or even reanalyze the problem. Once the program tests satisfactorily, it can be executed with real data, and solutions become available.

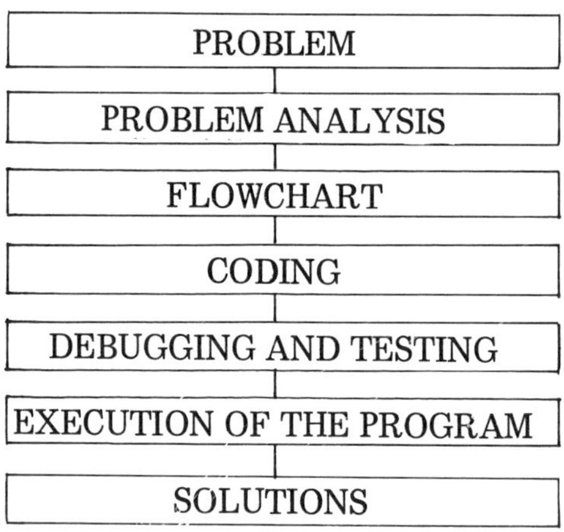

Figure 4-1

The problem analysis to be performed depends to some extent on the nature of the problem. Many business problems are mainly input/output related. In these cases, the problem analysis will also focus on input and output. For example, accounting reports may be generated or invoices printed. Many engineering problems, however, are more computational in nature, and the output may only consist of a few numbers. Under these conditions, the analysis of the problem focuses on the algorithms to be used. Consider the problem of solving the quadratic equation

$$AX^2 + BX + C = 0 \quad (A \neq 0)$$

Let X1, X2 be the roots of the equation. Three cases are possible:

1. $B^2 - 4AC < 0 \rightarrow$ no real roots exist
2. $B^2 - 4AC = 0 \rightarrow X1 = X2 = -B/(2A)$
3. $B^2 - 4AC > 0 \rightarrow X1 = \dfrac{-B + \sqrt{B^2 - 4AC}}{2A}$

$$X2 = \frac{-B - \sqrt{B^2 - 4AC}}{2A}$$

4.3 Flowcharting

After the problem has thus been analyzed, a flowchart can be drawn to show the logical flow of the program. A flowchart is a graphical representation of the program which assists the programmer in organizing the logic as well as the details of the program. It is a valuable part of the documentation and enables a person other than the programmer to use and maintain the program with minimal difficulty.

Standard flowcharting symbols are used to make the documentation useful to persons other than the programmer. The most frequently encountered symbols are shown in figure 4-2. All programs, whether the programmer is using BASIC or another programming language, utilize the standard symbols.

To illustrate the use of the symbols, the quadratic equation problem has been flowcharted (see figure 4-3). If A = 0, the equation is linear and not quadratic. This serves as a signal to terminate the program. The other two decisions are necessary to determine which of the three conditions — no, one, or two real roots — exists and which part of the program should be executed. Finally, all paths come together, and control is transferred back to the beginning of the program.

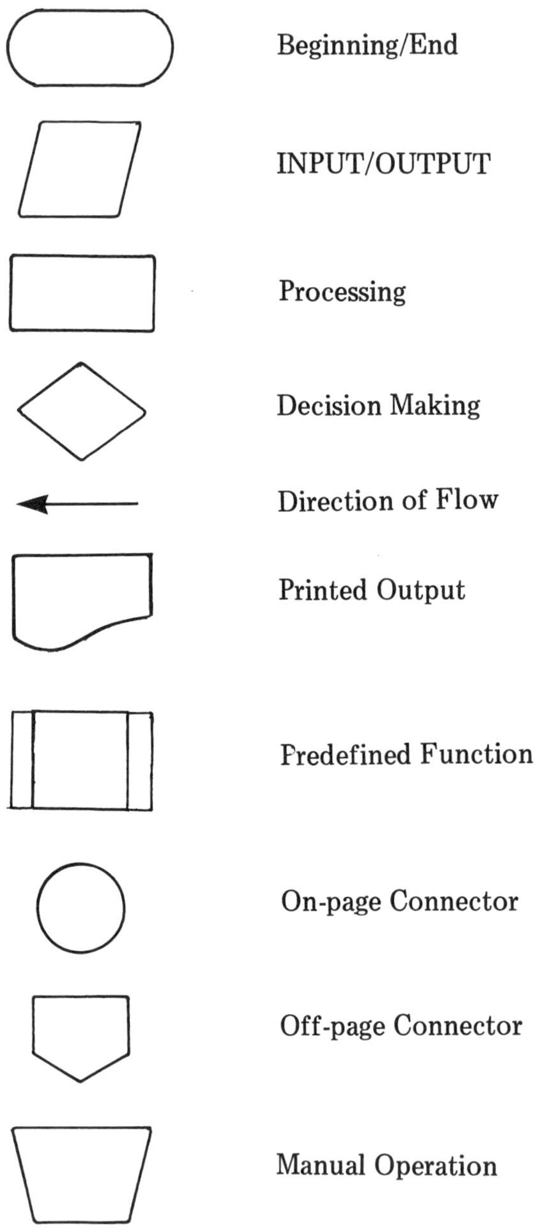
Beginning/End
INPUT/OUTPUT
Processing
Decision Making
Direction of Flow
Printed Output
Predefined Function
On-page Connector
Off-page Connector
Manual Operation

Figure 4-2

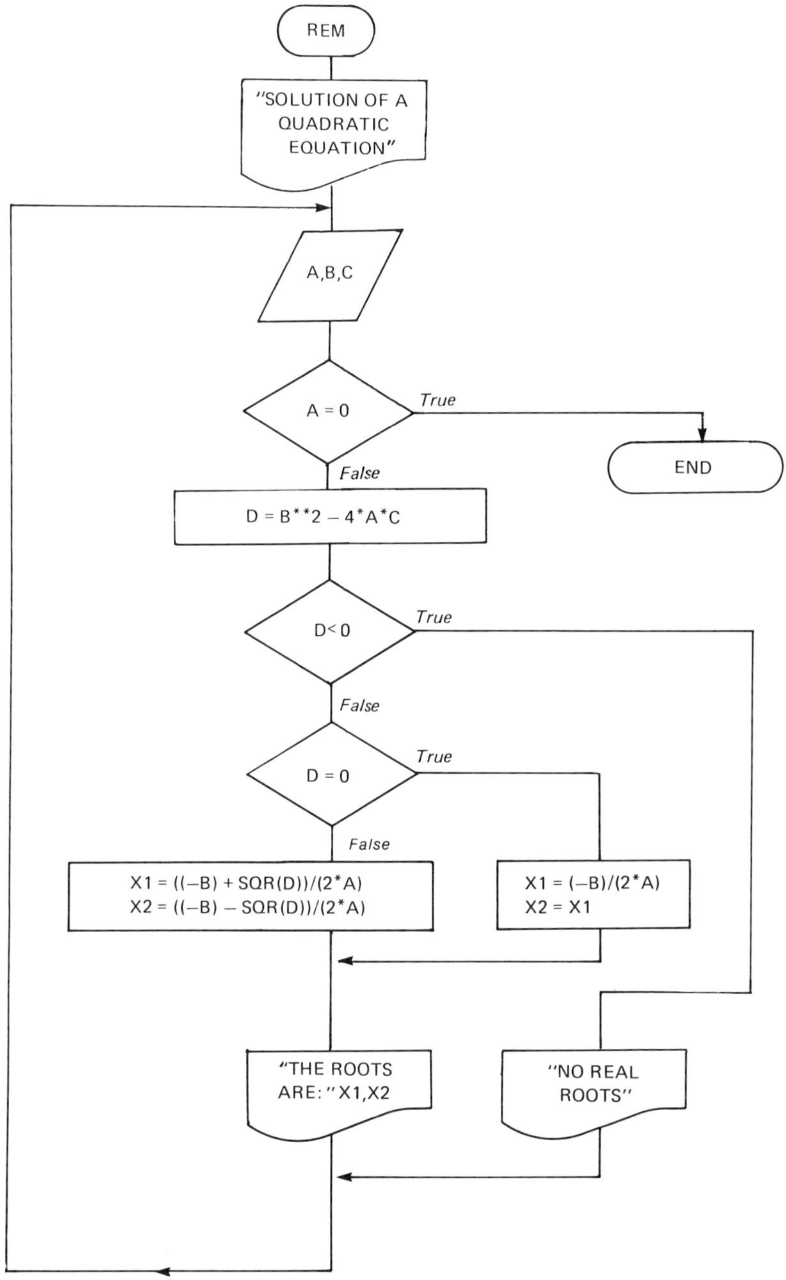
REM
"SOLUTION OF A QUADRATIC EQUATION"
A,B,C
A = 0
True
END
False
D = B**2 − 4*A*C
D< 0
True
False
D = 0
True
False
X1 = ((−B) + SQR(D))/(2*A)
X2 = ((−B) − SQR(D))/(2*A)
X1 = (−B)/(2*A)
X2 = X1
"THE ROOTS ARE: " X1,X2
"NO REAL ROOTS"

Figure 4-3

Another sample problem is the finding of the greatest common divisor of two positive integers. If M and N are two positive integers, D is a potential divisor and G is the greatest common divisor, the algorithm can be described as follows:

1. Let G = 1, D = N (or M whichever is smaller)
2. If M = N, then G = N (or M)
3. If M ≠ N, decrease D by 1
4. Test if both M and N are divisible by D by computing [1]
   T1 = INT (N/D) * D
   T2 = INT (M/D) * D
   If N = T1 and M = T2, then G = D, and the greatest common divisor has been found.
5. If either N ≠ T1 or M ≠ T2 or both check if D > 2.
   If not, print G. If yes, go back to 3.

The flowchart for this problem is shown in figure 4-4. Again, in a meaningful problem M ≠ 0; therefore, M = 0 leads to a termination of program execution. As in the previous flowchart, after printing of results, control is transferred back to the beginning so that more than one pair of numbers can be processed. The rest of the flowchart follows the problem analysis; the reader should compare the flowchart and algorithm to make sure he or she understands the flowcharting principles.

By now the reader should have an understanding of the function of the transfer-of-control statements. These statements will be discussed in detail the following sections.

4.4 The GO TO Statement

The GO TO statement causes an unconditional transfer of control. Its general form is

$$n_1 \text{ GO TO } n_2$$

where n_1 is the number of the GO TO statement and n_2 is the number of the statement to which control is to be transferred. Statement n_2 will be executed immediately after statement n_1 regardless of the relative position of the two statements in the program.

It should be obvious to the reader that $n_1 \neq n_2$. The statement

150 GO TO 150

would create an endless program which would accomplish nothing.

---

[1] Remember that INT (X) = largest integer ≤X

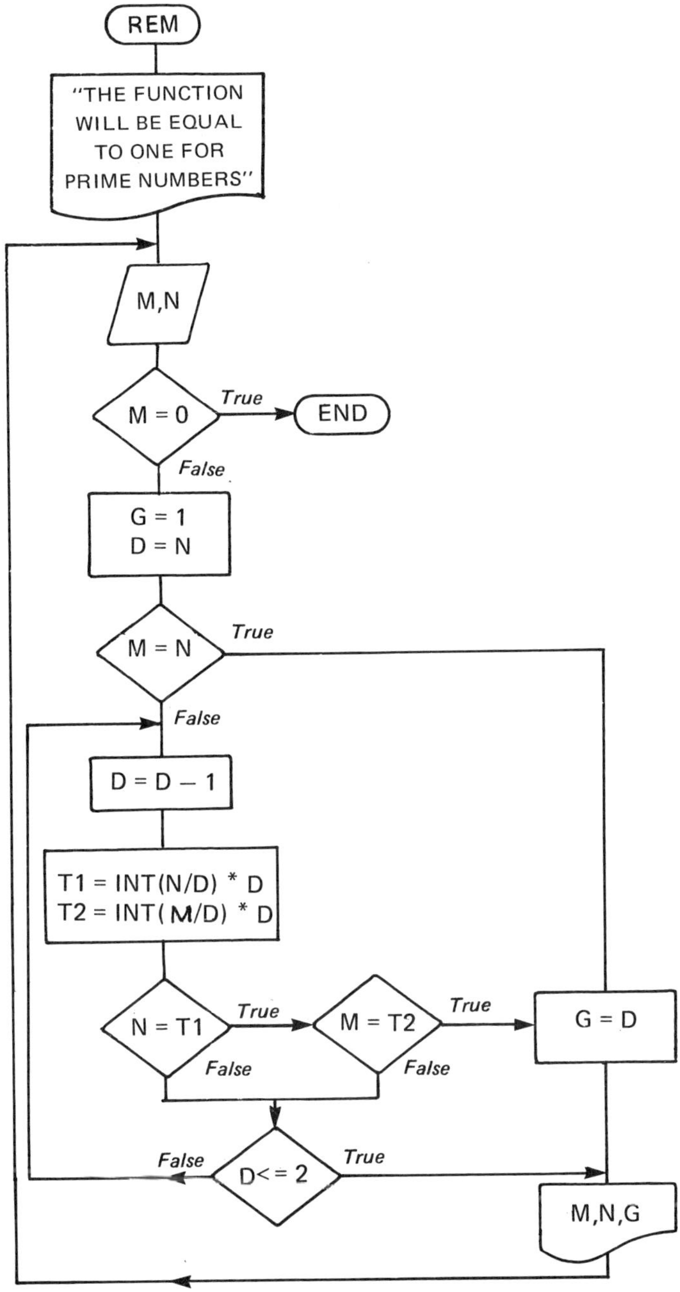
REM
"THE FUNCTION WILL BE EQUAL TO ONE FOR PRIME NUMBERS"
M,N
M = 0
True
END
False
G = 1
D = N
M = N
True
False
D = D − 1
T1 = INT(N/D) * D
T2 = INT(M/D) * D
N = T1
True
False
M = T2
True
False
G = D
False
D< = 2
True
M,N,G

Figure 4-4

Statement 150 would be executed continuously until the program is killed from the outside; the program will not come to an end of its own.

The GO TO statement will be illustrated in the computation of the distance between two points. If D is the distance and the coordinates of the two points are (X1, Y1) and (X2, Y2), then

$$D = \sqrt{(X1-X2)^2 + (Y1 - Y2)^2}$$

Figure 4-5 shows the flowchart of a program to compute the distance of pairs of points. The program is executed repeatedly until all the data are exhausted; at that point, an OUT OF DATA message is printed and the program is terminated (see chapter 2).

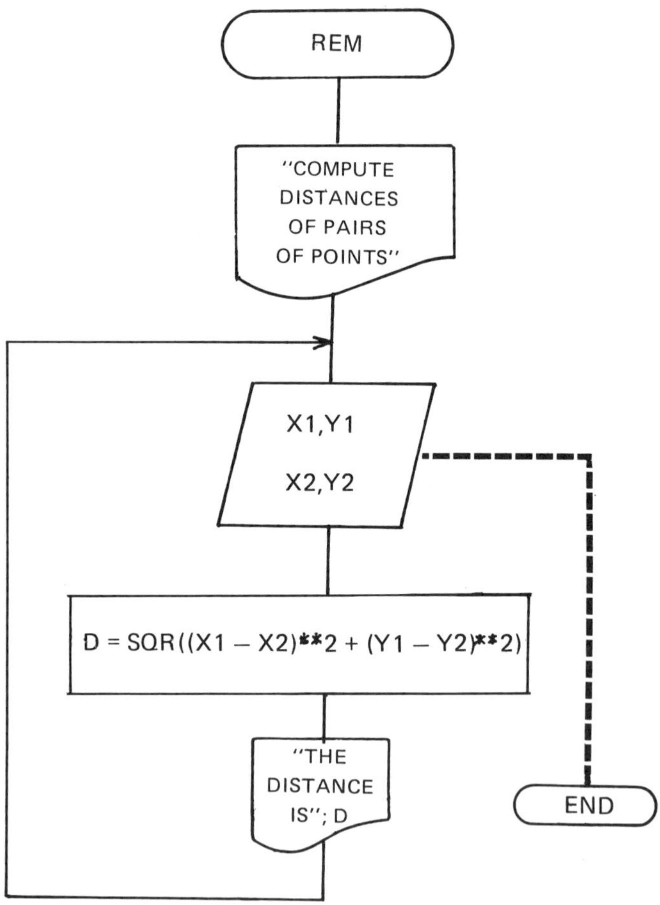

Figure 4-5

The program that corresponds to the flowchart in figure 4-5 is shown in figure 4-6. Note that the GO TO statement transfers control to statement 50. The headings need to be printed only once; consequently, the PRINT statements 20 through 40 are skipped on the second and later passes through the program.

```
10 REM THIS PROGRAM COMPUTES THE DISTANCE BETWEEN 2 POINTS
20 PRINT "THE DISTANCE BETWEEN 2 POINTS"
30 PRINT
40 PRINT "(X1 , Y1)", "(X2 , Y2)", "DISTANCE"
50 READ X1,Y1
60 READ X2,Y2
70 LET D = SQR((X1-X2)**2 + (Y1-Y2)**2)
80 PRINT "("; X1; ","; Y1; ")", "(";X2;",";Y2;")",D
90 GO TO 50
100 DATA 2,1
110 DATA 6,8
120 DATA 3,2
130 DATA 5,7
140 END

Ready
RUN

BKEXER.P7       10:46


THE DISTANCE BETWEEN 2 POINTS

(X1 , Y1)       (X2 , Y2)       DISTANCE
( 2 , 1 )       ( 6 , 8 )        8.06226
( 3 , 2 )       ( 5 , 7 )        5.38516

? Out of DATA in line 50
```

Figure 4-6

4.5 IF Statement

The IF statement causes a conditional transfer of control. It has the general form

$$n_1 \text{ IF } \langle \text{logical expression} \rangle \text{ THEN } n_2 \quad (1)$$

$$n_1 \text{ IF } \langle \text{logical expression} \rangle \text{ GO TO } n_2 \quad (2)$$

where n_1 is the number of the IF statement, n_2 is the number of the statement to which control is to be transfered. "Logical expression" will be explained in section 4.5.1. As was explained for the GO TO statement, $n_1 \neq n_2$ always or the program may stay permanently on statement n_2.

There is an alternative form for the IF statement:

n IF logical expression THEN<statement> (3)

where "logical expression" is explained in section 4.5.1 and "statement" is any executable statement.

The logical expression is a condition that can be either true or false. If the condition is true, control will be transferred or the statement at the end will be executed, depending on the form of statement used. If the logical expression is false, control passes on to the next statement in the normal program sequence, and the remainder of the IF statement is ignored.

4.5.1 Logical Expressions

In its most general form, a logical expression looks like this

⟨expression⟩⟨relational operator⟩⟨expression⟩

"Expression" can be a constant, a variable, or an arithmetic expression; both numeric and string constants and variables can be used. A relational operator is one of the following:

< less than
<= less than or equal to
= equal to
> greater than
>= greater than or equal to
<> not equal to

Some examples of logical expressions are shown in figure 4-7.

A = 6
X<> 9
N > M
3 * N > = Y + W
A$ = "YES"

Figure 4-7

All variables used in the logical expression should have had a value assigned to them earlier, either in a READ or a LET statement. If not, the value will be 0 on some systems and may be unpredictable on others. Only variables, constants, and expressions of the same type (numeric or string) can be compared.

Logical expressions are evaluated as follows:

1. Reduce the expressions on both sides of the relational operator to a constant. For example, if N = 4, Y = 2 and W = 3, then 3 * N = 12 and Y + W = 5.
2. The two expressions are compared. The result is either a "true" or a "false," depending on the relational operator used in the expression. For example, 12> = 5 is true. If the logical expression has been 3 * N < Y + W, the result would have been "false" because 12 < 5 is *not true*.

4.5.2 Illustrations of the IF Statement

Based on the evaluation of logical expressions explained above, an IF statement can be diagrammed as follows:

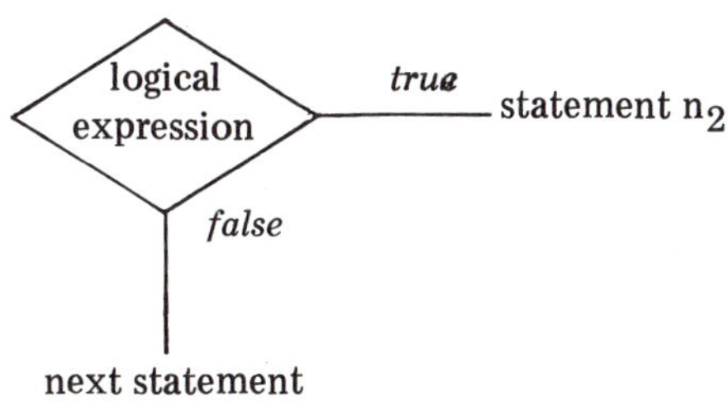

An example of an IF statement is shown in the flowchart and program segments in figure 4-8.

The program segment on the left shows version (1) of the IF statement. Note that a GO TO follows the IF; without it, statement 80 would be executed regardless of the value of W − Y.

The program segment on the right uses version (3) of the IF statement. Note that this segment is only three statements long as compared to five statements in the earlier version. Since nothing needs to be done when the statement is false, it is more economical to add the statement to the IF statement. If two or more statements would be necessary for both possible outcomes of the logical expression, the first version must be used.

We are now ready to write the programs for the problems which were analyzed and flowcharted earlier. The flowchart for the solving of quadratic equations was given in figure 4-3. The corresponding program is shown in figure 4-9.

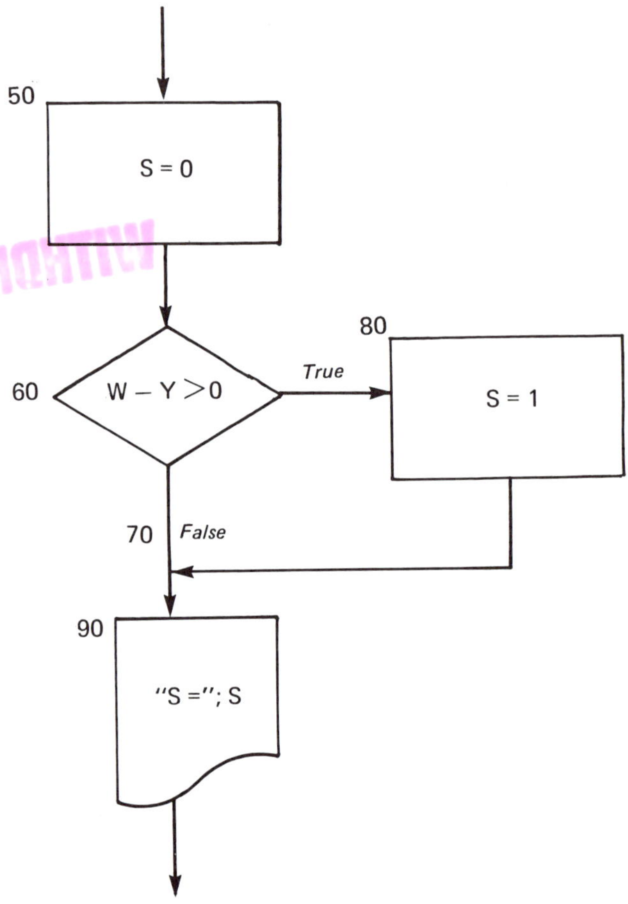


```
50  LET S =  0
60  IF W-Y > 0 THEN 80
70  GO TO 90
80  LET S =  1
90  PRINT "S = "; S
```

```
50  LET S = 0
60  IF W - Y > 0 THEN S = 1
90  PRINT "S = "; S
```

Figure 4-8

```
10 REM SOLVING SYSTEMS OF QUADRATIC EQUATIONS
20 PRINT "SOLUTIONS TO QUADRATIC EQUATIONS,"
25 PRINT "USING X2 AS A SQUARE"
30 PRINT
40 READ A,B,C
50 IF A=0 THEN 250
60 D = B ** 2 - 4 * A * C
70 IF D < 0 THEN 160
72 IF D=0 THEN 93
80 X1 = (-B - SQR(D))/(2*A)
90 X2 = (-B + SQR(D))/(2*A)
91 GOTO 100
93 X1=(-B)/(2*A)
94 X2=X1
100 PRINT A;" (X2) + "; B;" (X) + ";C;" = 0"
110 PRINT
120 PRINT "The roots are "X1" and "X2
130 PRINT "________________________________________"
140 PRINT
150 GO TO 40
160 PRINT A;" (X2) + ";B;" (X) + ";C;" = 0"
170 PRINT
180     PRINT "THE ROOTS ARE COMPLEX"
190 PRINT "________________________________________"
200 GO TO 40
210 DATA 5,-10,1
220 DATA 2,4,0
222 DATA 5,3,-26
230 DATA 1,2,3
240 DATA 0,0,0
250 END

Ready
RUNNH


SOLUTIONS TO QUADRATIC EQUATIONS,
USING X2 AS A SQUARE

 5  (X2) + -10  (X) +  1  = 0

The roots are  0.105573  and  1.89443
________________________________________

 2  (X2) +  4  (X) +  0  = 0

The roots are -2  and  0
________________________________________

 5  (X2) +  3  (X) + -26  = 0

The roots are -2.6  and  2
________________________________________

 1  (X2) +  2  (X) +  3  = 0

THE ROOTS ARE COMPLEX
________________________________________
```

Figure 4-9

Note the two IF statements (70 and 72). If $D < 0$, control is transferred to statement 160 and a message is printed; but no computations are performed since the square root of a negative number cannot be taken in the program. If D is not less than 0, it could be equal to or greater than 0. Therefore, a second IF statement follows immediately. If $D = 0$, control is transferred to statement 93 and the simplified formula is used. If the conditions were not met in either IF statement, D has to be greater than 0. No additional test is necessary at this point, and the general formula for solving quadratic equations is used.

A flowchart for the finding of the greatest common divisor was presented in figure 4-4. The corresponding program is shown in figure 4-10.

Note that control is transferred to statement 90 during the process of finding the greatest common divisor, that the initial values for G and D need to be set only once, and that $M \neq N$, or statements 90 through 160 would not have been executed the first time through.

When the greatest common divisor has been found and printed, control is transferred back to statement 40 to read in a new pair of values. At this time, it is necessary to set G and D back to their starting values and check if $M = N$.

4.5.3 The Compounded IF

The algorithm for the finding of the greatest common divisor requires that N =T1 and M = T2 for D to be a common divisor. In the program, this joint condition has been broken down into two sequential conditions — IF N = T1 then we check IF M = T2.

In many versions of BASIC, it is possible to check both of these relationships with just one IF statement — the compounded IF. The general form for this statement is

$$n_1 \quad \text{IF} \quad \langle \text{logical operation} \rangle \quad \text{THEN } n_2 \text{ or} \quad \langle \text{statement} \rangle$$

where n_1, n_2 are statement numbers and a logical operation has the form

$$\langle \text{logical expression} \rangle \ \langle \text{logical operator} \rangle \ \langle \text{logical expression} \rangle$$

Logical expressions are explained in section 4.5.1. Logical operators are AND, OR, NOT, XOR, IMP, and EQU. The meaning of these operators is summarized in figure 4-11.

```
10       REM FIND THE GREATEST COMMON DIVISOR
20       REM OF TWO NUMBERS
30       PRINT
40       READ M,N
50       IF M=0 GOTO 250
60       LET G = 1
70       LET D = N
80       IF M = N THEN 170
90       LET D = D - 1
100      LET T1 = INT(N/D)*D
110      LET T2 = INT(M/D)*D
120      IF N = T1 THEN 140
130      GO TO 150
140      IF M = T2 THEN 170
150      IF D < 2 GO TO 180
160      GO TO 90
170      LET G = D
180      PRINT "THE GREATEST COMMON DIVISOR OF"
190      PRINT  M;"AND";N"IS";G
200      PRINT
210      GOTO 40
220      DATA 24,36
230      DATA 16,25
240      DATA 0,0
250      END

Ready
RUN

BKEXER.P5M     11:14




THE GREATEST COMMON DIVISOR OF
 24 AND 36 IS 12

THE GREATEST COMMON DIVISOR OF
 16 AND 25 IS 1
```

Figure 4-10

Operator	Example	Resulting Value
AND	**E1 AND E2**	True if both E1 and E2 are true
OR	**E1 OR E2**	True if either E1 or E2 or both are true
NOT	**NOT E1**	True if E1 is false
XOR	**E1 XOR E2**	True if either E1 or E2 is true, but not both
IMP	**E1 IMP E2**	False if and only if E1 is true and E2 is false
EQU	**E1 EQU E2**	True if E1 and E2 are both true or both false

Figure 4-11

The following examples illustrate some of the uses of these operators.

Example 1. The statements

```
 90 LET S = 0
100 IF A < B  AND B < C THEN S = A
110 PRINT S
```

would lead to the printing of S under any condition. However, the value of S would depend on the values of A, B, and C as follows:

$A < B, B \geqslant C \rightarrow S = 0$
$A < B, B < C \rightarrow S = A$
$A \geqslant B, B \geqslant C \rightarrow S = 0$
$A \geqslant B, B < C \rightarrow S = 0$

Example 2. The statements

```
110 LET S = 0
120 IF A < B EQU B < C THEN S = A
130 PRINT S
```

would lead to the printing of S. In this case, the value of S would be determined as follows:

$A < B, B \geqslant C \quad S = 0$
$A < B, B < C \quad S = A$
$A \geqslant B, B \geqslant C \quad S = A$
$A \geqslant B, B < C \quad S = 0$

Example 3. The statements

```
140 LET S = 0
150 IF NOT A < B THEN S = A
160 PRINT S
```

would lead to the printing of S as follows:

$A < B \quad S = 0$
$A \geqslant B \quad S = A$

since the expression $A < B$ is false when $A \geqslant B$ and the rest of the IF statement is executed only when NOT $A < B$ is true or $A > B$ is false.

4.6 Sample Program

The principles discussed in this chapter can all be illustrated in the example of a program to solve a pair of linear equations in two unknowns. Given two linear equations,

$$a_1 x + b_1 y = c_1$$
$$a_2 x + b_2 y = c_2$$

the solutions are given as

$$x = \frac{c_2 b_1 - c_1 b_2}{a_2 b_1 - a_1 b_2} \qquad y = \frac{a_2 c_1 - a_1 c_2}{a_2 b_1 - a_1 b_2}$$

But the system does not have one unique solution in all cases. For example, if the two equations are dependent (all coefficients of one equation are a multiple of the corresponding coefficients of the other equation), then $a_2 b_1 - a_1 b_2 = 0$ and x and y cannot be computed with the formulas given previously. All the points on the line $a_1 x + b_1 y = c_1$ solve the system of two linear equations in the dependent case.

Another problem that can occur is that the two equations are inconsistent; this is the case when $a_1 = ka_2$ and $b_1 = kb_2$, but $c_1 \neq kc_2$ or the equations represent parallel lines with different Y intercepts. Inconsistent equations have no solution.

In figure 4-12, 4-13, and 4-14 flowchart, program, and sample results are shown for a program to solve a predetermined number of systems of linear equations in two unknowns.

In this program, a new method is used to determine the end of program execution. In the earlier programs, a program ended either with an OUT OF DATA message, or a special trailer record was read in to indicate the end of the program. Here, the number of equation systems to be solved is read in (statement 40). A counter is set up (statement 70), incremented each time one system of equations has been solved (statement 340) and tested (statement 350). Since K was set equal to 1 originally, it will always indicate which equation will be solved (first, second, . . . , N^{th}), and the program ends when K > N.

The program uses a slightly different approach than explained earlier. In the case of two unknowns, X can be computed as $(c_1 - b_1 Y)/a_1$ which is a more intuitive approach. The method indicated earlier, however, translates more easily into the general case of n equations in n unknowns.

The test for the dependent case in the program is

170 IF D1 = 0 GO TO 270
270 IF E1 = 0 THEN 280

This could be replaced by

170 IF D1 = 0 AND E1 = 0 THEN 280
175 IF D1 = 0 AND E1 <> 0 THEN 310

Both sets of statements will lead to the same results; in the second case, the program would have one less statement since the GO TO in statement 275 is not necessary.

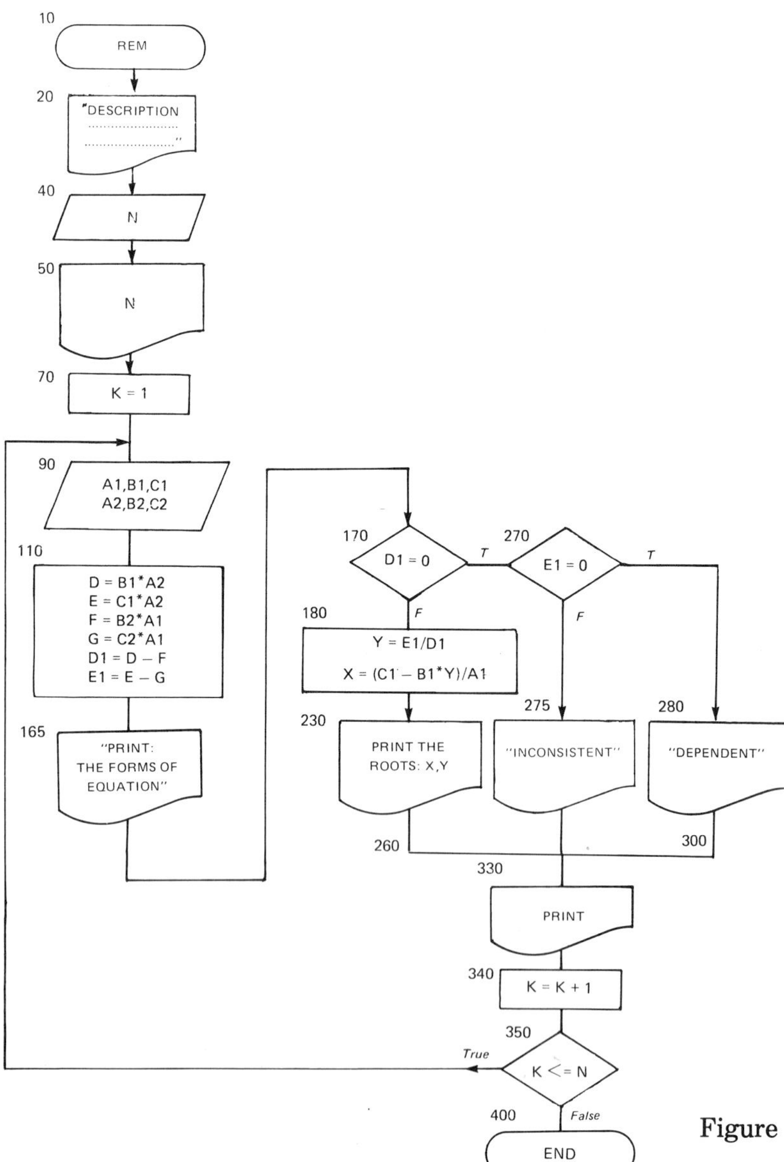

Figure 4-12

```
BKEXER.P4      11:15


10 REM SOLVING N PAIRS OF EQUATIONS WITH ERROR DETECTIONS.
20 PRINT "SOLVING N PAIRS OF EQUATIONS WITH ERROR DETECTIONS."
30 PRINT "IN THE FORM: A X + B Y = C"
40 READ N
50 PRINT "THERE ARE ";N;"PAIRS OF LINEAR EQUATIONS"
60 PRINT
70 LET K=1
90 READ A1,B1,C1
100 READ A2,B2,C2
110 D = B1 * A2
120 E = C1 * A2
130 F = B2 * A1
140 G = C2 * A1
150 D1 = D - F
160 E1 = E - G
165 PRINT A1;"(X) +";B1;"(Y) =";C1
166 PRINT A2;"(X) +";B2;"(Y) =";C2
167 PRINT
170 IF D1 = 0 GO TO 270
180 Y = E1/D1
190 X = (C1 - B1 * Y)/A1
230 PRINT "SET ";K;": X = "; X;, "Y = ";Y
240 PRINT "------------------------------------------------"
250 PRINT
260 GO TO 340
270 IF E1 = 0 THEN 280
275 GOTO 310
280 PRINT "SET "; K; ": THE EQUATIONS ARE DEPENDENT."
290 PRINT "------------------------------------------------"
300 GOTO 330
310 PRINT "SET "; K; ": THE EQUATIONS ARE INCONSISTENT."
320 PRINT "------------------------------------------------"
330 PRINT
340 LET K=K+1
350 IF K <= N THEN 90
360 DATA 3
370 DATA 2,4,6,8,10,12
380 DATA 1,1,2,2,2,4
390 DATA 2,5,10,2,5,8
400 END
```

Figure 4-13

```
BKEXER.F4        11:15



SOLVING N PAIRS OF EQUATIONS WITH ERROR
DETECTIONS. IN THE FORM: A X + B Y = C
THERE ARE  3 PAIRS OF LINEAR EQUATIONS

 2 (X) + 4 (Y) = 6
 8 (X) + 10 (Y) = 12

SET  1 : X = -1                 Y =  2
----------------------------------------------------

 1 (X) + 1 (Y) = 2
 2 (X) + 2 (Y) = 4

SET  2 : THE EQUATIONS ARE DEPENDENT.
----------------------------------------------------

 2 (X) + 5 (Y) = 10
 2 (X) + 5 (Y) = 8

SET  3 : THE EQUATIONS ARE INCONSISTENT.
----------------------------------------------------
```

Figure 4-14

EXERCISES

1. Identify and correct any errors in the statements below.
   a. **50 GO TO STOP**
   b. **60 GO TO 60**
   c. **70 GO TO 10**
   d. **100 READ A,B**
   e. **112 DATA 2,3**
   f. **120 DATA 5,8**
   g. **130 DATA 6,9**
   h. **140 LET C = (A + B)/2**
   i. **150 PRINT THE AVERAGE IS" C**
   j. **160 LET A + B = B /2 * 5**
   k. **170 GO TO 110**
   l. **180 END**

2. Identify and correct the errors that occur in some statements.
   a. 100 IF A > A$ THEN 150
   b. 110 IF X = Y GO TO 110
   c. 120 IF A + 4 =< 21 TO TO 200
   d. 125 IF A = 4 THEN GO TO 12
   e. 130 IF B + 2 * 3 = 30 GO TO 240
   f. 140 IF (C + B) * 2 > B$ THEN 260
   g. 150 IF M > N THEN PRINT M
   h. 160 IF (C **2 < 0) GO TO 280

3. Identify and correct the errors that occur in some statements.
   a. 170 IF (A OR B > 25) GO TO 300
   b. 180 IF (A * A = B AND B > C) GO TO 310
   c. 190 IF (A > B AND B > C) THEN A > C
   d. 200 IF (A + B < C OR A > C) THEN PRINT A
   e. 210 IF (NOT A < B) THEN G = A
   f. 220 IF (A$ = "YES" OR Q$ = "Y") GO TO 350

4. Given X = 8 and Y = 1, to which statement will the program branch as result of the following program segments?
   a. 30 IF X < Y THEN 80
      40 ...
   b. 30 IF X + Y < = Y * Y THEN 80
      40 ...
   c. 30 IF X/Y > = (X−1)*2 THEN 80
      40 ...
   d. 30 IF X > Y AND X < Y ** 2 THEN 80
      40 ...
   e. 30 IF Y * 2 < X OR X/Y > 2 THEN 80
      40 ...
   f. 30 IF NOT X * Y > Y ** 3 THEN 80
      40 ...

5. What is the output of the program below:

```
10 READ A
20 IF A * 2 >= 15 GO TO 50
30 PRINT A,
40 DATA 3,4,2,3.5,7.5,5.5
50 END
```

6. What are the results for each of the following program segments?
   a. 10 LET A = 5
      20 IF (A/2 > 2) GO TO 40
      30 GO TO 90

b.
```
10 LET B = 4
20 IF 12 * .5 < B GO TO 90
30 PRINT B
```

c.
```
10 LET C = 25
20 LET D = 18
30 IF C > D THEN 50
40 GO TO 90
50 PRINT C-D
```

7. Answer the following questions based on the program listed.

```
10 LET H = 0
20 READ N
30 IF N >= 999 GO TO 70
40 IF N < H GO TO 20
50 LET H = N
60 GO TO 20
70 PRINT N
80 DATA 23,43,12,64,63,999
90 END
```

   a. What does this program do?
   b. What will be the highest number expected?
   c. What is the importance of statement 10?
   d. What is the importance of statement 20?
   e. How many lines of output will there be?
   f. How will the output be?

8. Provide a flowchart for the program in problem 7.

9. Prepare a flowchart for a program that reads in two numbers and interchanges the values of the two numbers X and Y.

10. Prepare a flowchart to arrange a set of three number X, Y, Z in ascending order.

11. Develop a flowchart to compute

$$Y = \frac{C}{\tan \frac{x}{\sqrt{1 - x^2}}}$$

Make provisions for the case when the denominator is zero or undefined ( ).

12. Construct a flowchart to read two sets of numbers and merge them into one set. Then arrange the merged set in ascending order and print the output.

Programming Problems

1. Provide a BASIC program for Problem 9 with X = 25 and Y = 32.

2. Provide a program for problem 10 with X = 12, Y = 8, and Z = 10.

3. Provide a program for problem 11. Run it with your own data.

4. Develop a flowchart and computer program to solve problem 10, except arrange in descending order. Compare two numbers; if the first is smaller than the second number, then interchange, and repeat for the next pair of numbers. As the result X, Y, and Z are in descending order.

5

Transfer of Control — Looping

5.1 Introduction

Many engineering problems lead eventually to the evaluating of a polynomial or to the solving of an equation which requires iterative methods.

With the techniques developed so far, we could evaluate a polynomial of the form

$$Y = \sum_{i=0}^{n} a_i \ x^i$$

for any given value of n and coefficients a_0, a_1, —, a_n, by writing a LET statement. For example, for n = 3

```
700 LET Y = AO + A1*X + A2*X**2 + A3*X**3
```

would produce the desired result.

However, this is rather awkward if we have a larger n or if n could vary from one program execution to the next — in which case we would have to rewrite statement 700 for each new set of values. A better way is to use a technique known as looping — setting up a program segment that is executed n times where n can be entered at execution time. To do this, we would rewrite the polynomial as

$$y = (((a_n x + a_{n-1})\ x + a_{n-2})\ x + a_{n-3})\ x + \ldots + a_0$$

or, in the example for n = 3

$$y = ((a_3x + a_2)\,x + a_1)\,x + a_0$$

Now we have to compute a term of the form z = a x + b repeatedly, where the previously computed value always becomes the new a. The flow chart for the computation of y would be

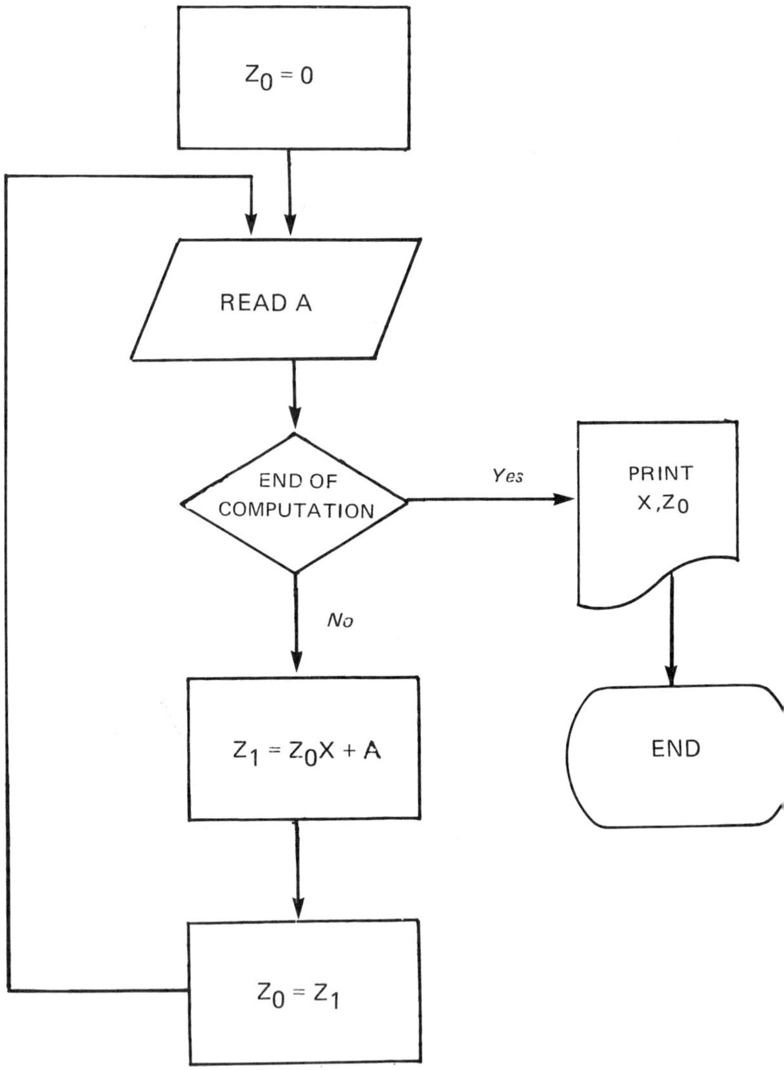

How can we write a program to solve this problem? There are actually two ways of doing this. One method uses the IF statement discussed in chapter 4 and will be discussed in section 5.2. In section 5.3, we will introduce two new statements, the FOR and NEXT statements, which will provide an easier way to program a loop. Two complete sample programs in section 5.4 will complete the discussion of loops.

5.2 Loops Using the IF Statement

The method outlined in the introduction for computing the value of a polynomial is an example of an iterative process. An iterative process generally involves 3 steps:

1. Initialization of the system. This includes setting up counters, determining starting values for numerical methods, and, in some cases, initializing a sum location to zero. The initialization step is executed only once.
2. Process (computations). This part may consist of one equation which is evaluated repeatedly, or of a whole series of computations that need to be done. This part will always be done repeatedly in the same manner, but with changing values of the variables.
3. End condition. The process part has to be executed a given number of times; a test has to be performed to determine when to cease processing, or the computer will execute the same loop indefinitely. We can diagram the loop in the following form:

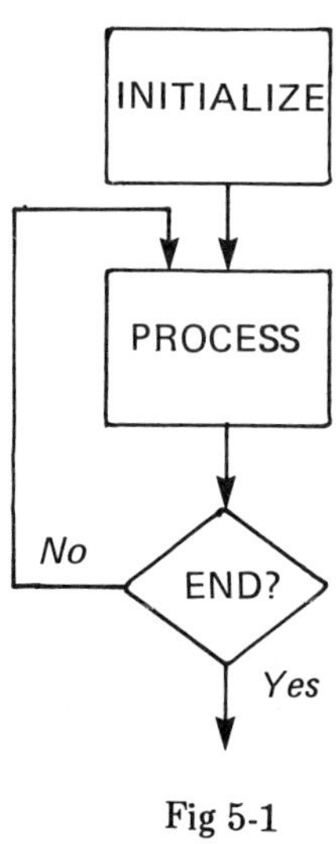

Fig 5-1

In the form presented in figure 5-1, the process will be executed at least once. In some cases, it may be worthwhile to determine at execution time if the process should be executed at all. In this case, the loop would be set up as shown in figure 5-2.

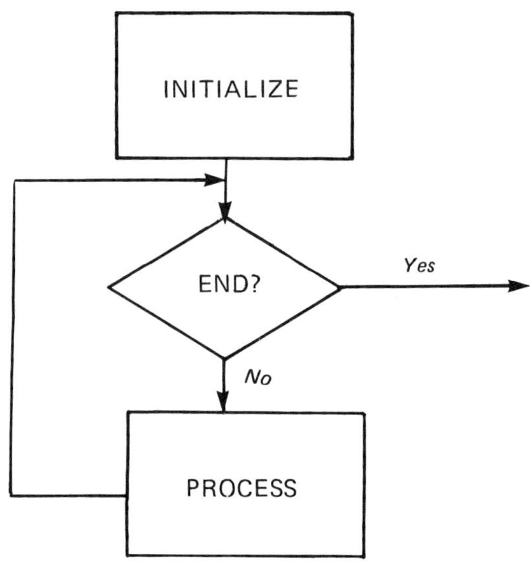

Figure 5-2

For the polynomial example discussed in section 5.1, the three phases of the loop would be

Initialize: Read X, N, A; set $Z_0 = A_n$, $C = 0$
Process: Read A
$Z_1 = Z_0 X + A$
$Z_0 = Z_1$
$C = C + 1$
End condition: $C = N$

With the statements discussed in the preceding chapters, we can write a program for the polynomial problem. The IF statement, combined with a GO TO as shown in the flowchart in figure 5-2, is adequate. We would set up the program as shown in figure 5-3.

```
100 READ X,N,ZO
110 LET C = 0
120 READ A
130 LET ZO = ZO*X + A
140 LET C = C + 1
150 IF C < N THEN 290
160 PRINT "X = ";X,"ZO = ";ZO
290 IF C < N THEN 120
370 DATA 2,4,1
380 DATA 1,1,1,5
390 END

Ready
RUN

POLY.01          11:27



X =  2           ZO =  35
```

Figure 5-3

One area has to be treated with caution. Depending on the location of the IF statement, the END test is C > N or C = N; for example, the program in figure 5-4 would yield the same results as the program in figure 5-3.

5.3 Loops Using the FOR and NEXT Statement

Although it is always possible to program a loop using the IF statement, it is not always very convenient, especially if there are several loops or if decisions requiring IF statements have to be made in the process part; program changes that require renumbering also may lead to confusion.

5.3.1 Single Loops

BASIC has two statements specifically for the programming of loops. These perform the initializing of the loop index and the end-of-loop check and set up the necessary counter. These statements are

```
240 READ X,N,ZO
250 LET C = 0
285 IF C = N THEN 360
290 READ A
300 LET ZO = ZO*X + A
310 LET C = C + 1
350 GO TO 285
360 PRINT "X = ";X,"ZO = ";ZO
370 DATA 2,4,1
380 DATA 1,1,1,5
390 END

Ready
RUN

POLY.02         11:27



X =  2          ZO =  35
```

Figure 5-4

n_1 FOR<index> = e_1 TO e_2 BY e_3

and

n_2 NEXT <index>

where n_1 and n_2 are statement numbers, index is the counter variable, and e_1 and e_2 are constants or variables defining the lower and upper limits of the index. The BY e_3 part is optional; if increments other than 1 are desired, this is specified in e_3.

Example:

100 FOR I = 1 TO 10

•

•

•

200 NEXT I

will cause the statements between 100 and 200 to be executed for I = 1, 2, 3, 4, 5, 6, 7, 8, 9, 10. The statements

```
100 FOR I = 1 TO 10 BY 2
        •
        •
200 NEXT I
```

will lead to only 5 passes through the process part, namely for I = 1, 3, 5, 7, 9. Using the FOR and NEXT statements, the program to evaluate the polynomial can be rewritten as shown in figure 5-5.

```
240 READ X,N,ZO
250 FOR I = 1 TO N
290 READ A
300 LET ZO = ZO*X + A
310 NEXT I
360 PRINT "X = ";X,"ZO = ";ZO
370 DATA 2,4,1
380 DATA 1,1,1,5
390 END

Ready
RUN

POLY.04          11:28



X =  2           ZO =  35
```

Figure 5-5

Having introduced the two new statements in an example, we can now discuss the elements of the statement in a little more detail. The index (I in the example) takes the part of the loop counter. Its value is incremented by e_3 after execution of the process part; if e_3 is not specified, it is taken to be 1.

The initial value e_1 (1 in the example) can be a numeric constant, a numeric variable, or an expression.

The test value e_2 (N in the example) can also be a numeric constant, variable, or expression. At the completion of each pass through the loop, the index is compared with e_2, and control passes to the statement following the NEXT statement if index $> e_2$ (for $e_3 > 0$) or index $<$ e_2 (for $e_3 < 0$).

The increment e_3 is added (algebraically) to the index after each execution of the statements in the loop. The phrase BY e_3 can be omitted, in which case the increment is 1.

The name used for the index in the NEXT statement has to be the same as that used in the FOR statement. The NEXT I statement in the example signals the end of the loop with index I; there might be other loops, and the index variable is used to distinguish between them. The NEXT statement transfers control back to the beginning of the loop and triggers the change in the index variable and testing for the end of the loop.

So far, we have discussed the simplest case of a loop. No decisions are made within the loop, and only one index is active at a given time. Both of these situations are not always given, and there are a few rules about loops that need to be added.

Let us write a program to check if a number N is a prime number.[1] N is a prime number if it is divisible by 1 and N only. It is not necessary to test if N is divisible by numbers $A > \sqrt{N}$ since $N/A < \sqrt{N}$, in that case, and a number less than A would have been found. N is divisible by A if

INT (N/A) * A = N

where INT (N/A) is the greatest integer $\leqslant$ N/A. Figure 5-6 shows a program to check if N is a prime number.

As it was set up, the program illustrates the possibility to transfer control out of the loop before the upper bound is reached. It is legitimate to do that. However, it is *not* possible to transfer control into the loop from outside its range. This is understandable since one would bypass the FOR statement, and the index would not be set up properly.

---

1 We are somewhat limited in our example since we have not discussed arrays; more meaningful examples will be discussed in chapter 6.

The program presented in figure 5-6 only finds the lowest number by which N is divisible. If it is desired to find all divisors of N which are less than $\sqrt{N}$, the program can be modified to print the divisor inside the loop and then check for additional divisors. An example is given in figure 5-7.

```
10 DATA 13,16,111,113
50 READ N
100 FOR I = 2 TO SQR(N)
200 LET A = N/I
300 IF INT(A)*I=N THEN 700
400 NEXT I
500 PRINT N, "IS A PRIME NUMBER"
600 GO TO 50
700 PRINT N, "IS DIVISIBLE BY",I
750 GO TO 50
800 END

Ready
RUN

PRIME              11:32

 13                IS A PRIME NUMBER
 16                IS DIVISIBLE BY                 2
 111               IS DIVISIBLE BY                 3
 113               IS A PRIME NUMBER

? Out of DATA in line 50
```

Figure 5-6

Note that statement 300 transfers control to the NEXT statement to increment the loop index; going back to 100 would initialize I and start the loop all over again and is, therefore, illegal.

The variable S is used to check if N is a prime number. If a divisor has been found, S is set to 1; otherwise, S = 0 when the loop is completed. To summarize, the rules for a single loop are as follows:

1. Each FOR statement has to have a matching NEXT statement, the two statements are connected through the index variable.
2. No statement within the range of the loop can redefine the parameters in the FOR statement (c_1, e_2, e_3).
3. Transfer of control is permissible within the loop or to the NEXT statement and/or to a statement outside the range of the loop. It is illegal to transfer control from outside the loop into the range of the loop.

```
10 DATA 13,16,111,113
50 READ N
60 PRINT
80 LET S = 0
100 FOR I = 2 TO N-1
200 LET A = N/I
300 IF INT(A)*I<N THEN 400
320 LET S = 1
330 PRINT N, "IS DIVISIBLE BY",I
400 NEXT I
450 IF  S = 1 GO TO 50
500 PRINT N, "IS A PRIME NUMBER"
600 GO TO 50
800 END

Ready
RUN

DIVIS           11:33



 13             IS A PRIME NUMBER

 16             IS DIVISIBLE BY                  2
 16             IS DIVISIBLE BY                  4
 16             IS DIVISIBLE BY                  8

 111            IS DIVISIBLE BY                  3
 111            IS DIVISIBLE BY                  37

 113            IS A PRIME NUMBER

? Out of DATA in line 50
```

Figure 5-7

5.3.2 Nested Loops

The program in figure 5-6 contains both a FOR NEXT loop (statement 100 through 400) and a loop controlled by, essentially, statements 50 and 600 or 750 (the program ends when the DATA block has been exhausted). It is an example of a *nested loop* — one loop within another loop. A program with a nested loop is shown in figure 5-8.

```
10   PRINT "START"
20   FOR I=1 TO 3
30   FOR J=1 TO 4
40   LET A=I+J
50   PRINT A, I, J
60   NEXT J, I
70   PRINT "MISSION ACCOMPLISHED"
80   END

Ready
RUN

DENN.03          10:34


START
 2             1              1
 3             1              2
 4             1              3
 5             1              4
 3             2              1
 4             2              2
 5             2              3
 6             2              4
 4             3              1
 5             3              2
 6             3              3
 7             3              4
MISSION ACCOMPLISHED
```

Figure 5-8

Note that the two loops are controlled by two different index variables. The outer loop is controlled by I and includes all statements between 20 and 60. The inner loop is controlled by J and includes all statements between 30 and 60.

The rules governing nested loops are an extension of those for the single loop and are listed below:

1. The index for each FOR NEXT statement pair has to be unique to allow unambiguous matching of the beginning and end of each loop.
2. The range of the inner loop must not extend beyond the range of the outer loop.

Illegal	**Legal**
FOR I	**FOR I**
FOR J	**FOR J**
NEXT I	**NEXT J**
NEXT J	**NEXT I**

3. Two or more loops may end on the same statement; the indices in the NEXT statement have to be listed so that the inner loop terminates first.

FOR I
FOR J
NEXT J, I

4. It is permissible to transfer control outside of the range of a loop, but not into the range of a loop, just as with single loops. However, this is somewhat more intricate for nested loops. Permissible and illegal transfers are illustrated below.

Permissible	**Impermissible**
FOR I	**FOR I**
FOR J	**FOR J**
NEXT J	**NEXT J**
NEXT I	**NEXT I**

5.4 Example

The programming of loops in BASIC will be illustrated through an example of an iterative process — solving a transcendental equation using the Newton-Raphson method.

Suppose we want to find a real number x to solve the equation $f(x) = 0$. In all except a few cases, there is no formula which will give us the exact solution; approximation methods have to be used. In this section, we will present Newton's method as an example. Newton's method involves three steps:[1]

1. Finding an approximate root. This can be done graphically (see figure 5-9). A rough graph of the function $y-f(x)$ yields a point (x_0, y_0) which is close to the exact root r.

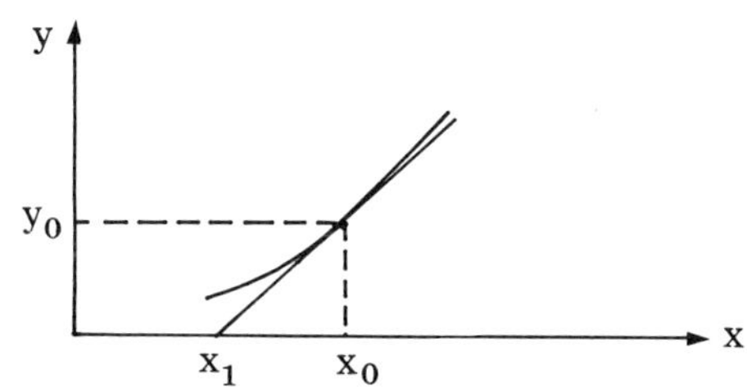

Figure 5-9

2. Finding a closer approximation x_1. This is found in the point where the tangent to the function at $(x_0, f(x_0))$ crosses the x-axis.

   As can be easily seen, $x_1 = x_0 - \frac{f(x_0)}{f'(x_0)}$

   The process does not work for a starting point with $f'(x_0) = 0$. If we happened to select such a value x_0, we need to find a nearby starting point.
3. Computing new approximations, using the formula

   $$x_{n+1} = x_n - \frac{f(x_n)}{f'(x_n)}$$

   After each step, we check how close our approximation is. The process terminates if

   $$|x_{n+1} - x_n| < \epsilon$$

   for a predetermined value of ε.

---

[1] See George P. Thomas Jr., *Calculus and Analytic Geometry*, Alternate Edition, Addison-Wesley Publishing Company, Reading, Mass., 1972, 463-467.

Newton's method does not always converge. It is, therefore, necessary to put a limit on the number of steps or to check if

$$|x_{n+1} - x_n| > |x_n - x_{n-1}|$$

to avoid never-ending loops.

A program to find the root of an equation using Newton's method is shown in figure 5-10. This program is written for a specific equation; $0 = x - .5e^{.5x}$. In a later chapter we will modify the program so that it works for any function f(x) (see chapter 8).

Statements 100-200 set the starting value ($x_0 = 0$), the accuracy criterion ($\varepsilon = .005$), and the maximum number of steps (N = 50). These parameters could be read in for a more general program.

The iterative process is contained in statements 200 through 280. The first derivative $f'(x) = 1 - .25e^{.5x}$ is computed for x_0 in statement 220; if $f'(x_0) < .0005$, the iteration is stopped because the slope is too close to 0 (statements 230, 320-340). The new value for x is computed in statement 240. Statements 250-260 check for convergence. Finally x_1 replaces x_0 in statement 270, and another iterative step starts.

Table 5-1 indicates the number of steps needed to convergence for different starting points. This indicates that the process is quite robust; the starting value does not really have to be close in many cases. However, if the equation has several roots, the process might converge to another root if the starting value is chosen carelessly.

Table 5-1

Steps to convergence for different values of x_0*

x_0	No. of steps
−1	3
0	3
1	3
2	4
2.5	5

*The root is at x = .7148; the next larger root is found at 4.3066

```
10   REM   ****************************
20   REM   PROGRAM TO SOLVE THE
30   REM   EQUATION    X = .5*EXP(.5*X)
40   REM   USING NEWTON'S METHOD
50   REM   ****************************
100  LET X0 = 0
110  LET E0 = .005
120  LET N = 50
200  FOR I = 1 TO N
210  LET F = X0 - .5*EXP(.5*X0)
220  LET F1 = 1 - .25*EXP(.5*X0)
230  IF ABS(F1) < .0005 THEN 320
240  LET X1 = X0 - F/F1
250  LET E1 = ABS(X0 - X1)
260  IF E1 < E0 THEN 360
270  LET X0 = X1
280  NEXT I
290  PRINT "AFTER ";N;" STEPS NO CONVERGENCE"
300  PRINT "X0 = " X0, "E1 = " E1
310  GO TO 900
320  PRINT "SLOPE = 0 AT X0 = ";X0
330  PRINT "START AGAIN WITH DIFFERENT X0"
340  GO TO 900
360  PRINT "CONVERGENCE REACHED AFTER"
370  PRINT I, "STEPS"
380  PRINT "X = " X1, "EPSILON = " E1
900  END

Ready
RUN

NEWTON          10:14



CONVERGENCE REACHED AFTER
 3              STEPS
X =  0.714806 EPSILON =  3.12932E-4
```

Figure 5-10

EXERCISES

1. Provide a BASIC statement or program segment for each of the following:
   a. Transfer control to statement 90 if K is greater than 50.
   b. If the variable A$ has a value of YES, branch to statement 20.
   c. Let K be the counter. Write the necessary statements such that when the counter exceeds 30, branch out to statement 900, otherwise increase the counter and branch back to statement 80 to repeat the looping.
   d. Code the flowchart below:

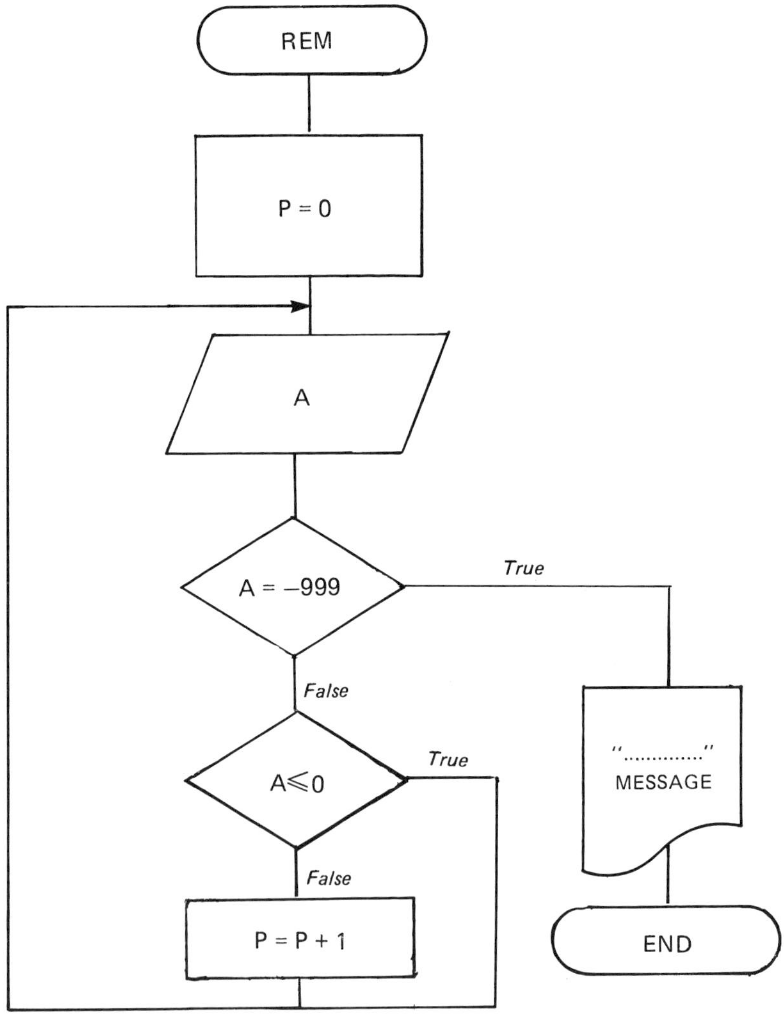

e. What has problem (d) accomplished? What do the variables P, A represent?

f. Code the flowchart below:

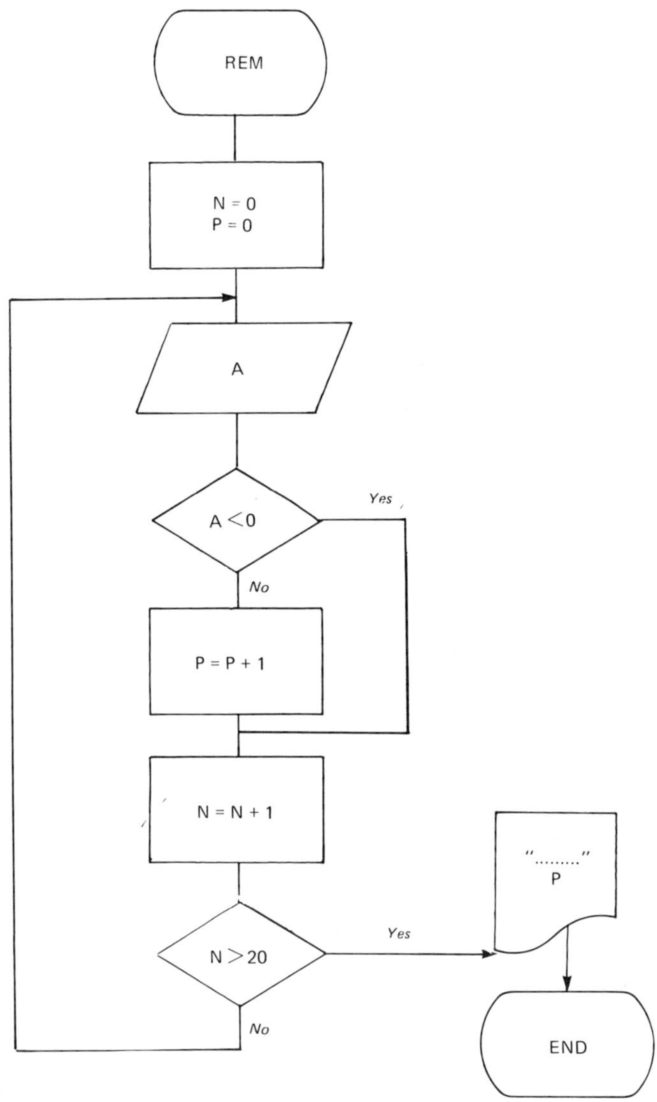

g. What has (f) accomplished? What do the variables N, P and A represent?

2. Determine the number of times the loop will be executed:
   a. 50 FOR I = 1 TO 13
   b. 50 FOR J = 1 TO 9 BY 2
   c. 50 FOR K = 2 TO 15 BY 2
   d. 50 FOR L = 1 TO 5 BY .5
   e. 50 FOR M = 20 TO 9 BY −2

3. Determine the value of the output after each of the following program segments is executed:

   a.
```
106 LET S = 1
110 LET N = 5
120 LET I = 1 TO N
130 LET S = S * I
140 NEXT I
150 PRINT S
```

   b.
```
100 LET S = 0
110 FOR I = 1 TO 10 BY 2
120 LET S = S + 1
130 NEXT I
140 PRINT I , S
```

   c.
```
100 LET J = 4
110 LET K = 3
120 FOR I = 1 TO J + K BY 2
130 LET L = I * I
140 PRINT I , L
150 NEXT I
```

   d.
```
100 LET T = 0
110 LET P = 2
120 LET Q = 3
130 LET N = 4
140 FOR I = 0 TO N
150 LET T = T + 1/(P+I*Q)
160 PRINT I , T
170 NEXT I
```

   e.
```
100 LET R = 4
110 LET S = 2
120 FOR I = 8 TO 9 BY S
130 LET W = I + S + R
```

```
140 IF W >= 12 THEN 160
150 NEXT I
160 LET W = W * 2
180 PRINT I , W
```

4. Identify the errors, if any, in each of the following program segments:

a.
```
20 FOR I = 1 TO 10
30 LET I = I * 2
40 PRINT I
50 NEXT I
```

b.
```
10 LET S = 0
20 FOR J = 1 TO 20
30 LET K = SQR(J)
40 LET S = S + K
50 NEXT S
```

c.
```
10 FOR N = 1 TO 20
20 LET N2 = N ** 2
30 IF N2 >= 50 GO TO 60
40 PRINT N , N2
50 NEXT N
60 STOP
```

d.
```
10 LET S = 0
20 FOR M = 1 TO 20
30 LET L = M * 2
40 IF L > 30 GO TO 70
50 LET S = S + L
60 NEXT M
70 PRINT "THE NUMBER IS TOO LARGE"
80 GO TO 50
```

e.
```
10 LET S = 0
20 FOR A$ = 1 TO 10
30 LET S = S + A$
40 NEXT A$
50 PRINT S
```

5. Calculate the output of this program.

```
10 FOR A = 1 TO 5
20 FOR B = 1 TO 5
30 LET C = SQR ( A**2 + B**2 )
40 PRINT A, B, C
50 NEXT B
60 NEXT A
70 END
```

   a. What does this program accomplish?
   b. Describe an application of this program.
   c. How would the output change if statement 20 is changed to

      20 FOR B = A + 1 TO 5

6. Consider the following program

```
100 FOR I = 1 TO 4
110 LET L = 999E10
120 FOR J = 1 TO 3
130 READ N
140 IF L <= N THEN 160
150 L = N
160 NEXT J
170 PRINT "L HAS A VALUE OF"; L
180 NEXT I
190 DATA 2, 9, 3, 8, 4, 7, 5, 6, 8, 9, 4, 5
200 END
```

   a. How many lines of output will this program generate?
   b. Interpret this output in a narrative form.
   c. What would the output be if statement 170 and statement 180 were interchanged?
   d. What would be the effect of changing statement 110 to 110 LET L = 0?
   e. What would be the effect of changing statement 110 as in (d) and statement 140 to 140 IF L >= N THEN 160?

7. Identify and correct the errors, if any, in the following programs:

a.
```
10 FOR I = 1 TO 10
20 FOR J = 1 TO 20
30 LET P = I * J
40 PRINT I, J, P
50 NEXT I
60 NEXT J
70 END
```

b.
```
10 FOR R = 1 TO 3
20 READ N
30 DATA 2
40 FOR C = 1 TO N
50 LET R = R + C
60 PRINT " R = " ; R
70 NEXT C
80 NEXT R
90 END
```

Programming Problems

1. Construct a program that calculates the total elapsed time (T) and function value g(t) of the function

$$g(t) = 1 - e^{-t}$$

where t = 0 through 5 with increment of .5.

2. Write a program for a popular mathematical problem, the Fibonacci sequence. The Fibonacci sequence is that the first two numbers are 1 and the next following is obtained by summing the two preceding numbers, such that the sequence appears as:

1, 1, 2, 3, 5, 8, ...

Print the first 20 numbers with 5 numbers on each line.

3. Construct a program to calculate the sum of a series until the difference between two consecutive values of S is less than .00005. If this has not been accomplished after a certain number of terms has been calculated and added to the sum, a message should be printed out. For this particular problem use the series as:

$$S(x) = x - \frac{x^3}{3} + \frac{x^5}{5} + \frac{x^7}{7} + \frac{x^9}{9} + \ldots$$

4. Construct a program to do the same as in problem 3 by using the function as:

$$S(x) = x - \frac{x^2}{4} + \frac{x^3}{9} + \frac{x^4}{16} + \frac{x^5}{25} + \ldots$$

6

Subscripted Variables

Introduced in the preceding chapters were a number of statements that allow the user to handle a large number of computational problems in BASIC. This and the following chapters serve to expand the reader's knowledge of BASIC by introducing additional features that will make programs more efficient and the output more convenient.

Up to now, every variable name represented a single value and was assigned to a single storage location. If a problem required the handling of 10 variables simultaneously, 10 variable names had to be assigned and this made programs rather unwieldy in many cases.

Variables which are logically related, such as the coordinates of a point in n-dimensional space, are frequently grouped together in a vector or array. In algebra, the elements of a vector X are indicated by subscripts: $X = (X_1, X_2, \ldots, X_n)$.

It is possible to use subscripted variables in BASIC, and special statements are available for the definition and manipulation of vectors and matrices. These statements will be presented in section 6.2 and those following it. In section 6.1, an example is introduced which would require an inordinate amount of coding without the use of subscripted variables; the program for this example will be presented in figure 6-7 later in the chapter.

6.1 Sort Routine

The purpose of a sort routine is to sort data in ascending or descending order. There are several sorting techniques which are frequently used.

Conceptually the simplest is the bubble sort which is demonstrated in this section.

Let X be the array that needs to be sorted, X containing elements $X_1, X_2, \ldots, X_n$. Let T be a temporary location to be used in the sort. The algorithm for the bubble sort is outlined in the following problem analysis and the flowchart in figure 6-1. The procedure can be described as follows:

1. Compare the first value in the array (X_1) to all the remaining values ($X_2, X_3, \ldots, X_n$).
   - i. If one of these values is smaller than X_1, interchange the two values, and proceed.
   - ii. If not, leave the array unchanged.

   When the complete list has been examined, the smallest value has floated to the top.
2. Now compare the second value in the array to all remaining values, following the same procedure as outlined under 1. At the end of the second pass through the array, the second smallest value will have been moved into the second position in the array.
3. This process is repeated to obtain the third, fourth, . . ., smallest value.

   A total of N-1 passes through the array are necessary to sort N values.

For example, suppose the list contains four values: $X_1 = 3$, $X_2 = 1$, $X_3 = 6$, $X_4 = 2$. The data will be sorted as indicated, where ↕ means compare and exchange the values and ↘ means compare, but do not exchange.

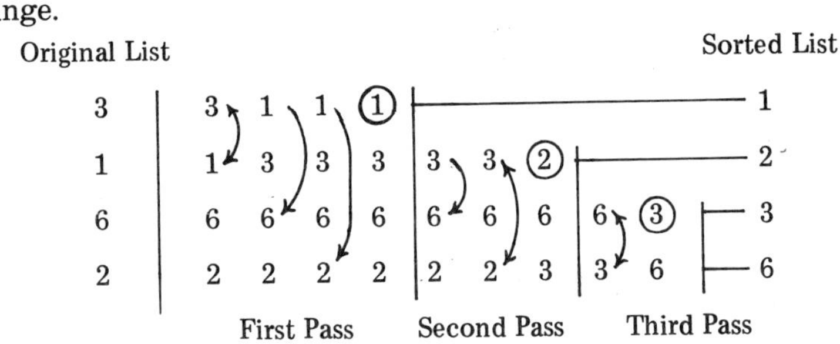

With four variables in this example, three passes through the data are necessary, and each time the names of the variables in the array are referenced. If simple variables are used, it is necessary to keep track of the names for N different variables, and the program will become very large. However, a problem such as this is feasible to solve in a computer program when subscripted variables are available. In the remainder of chapter 6, the use of subscripted variables and matrix operations will be explained.

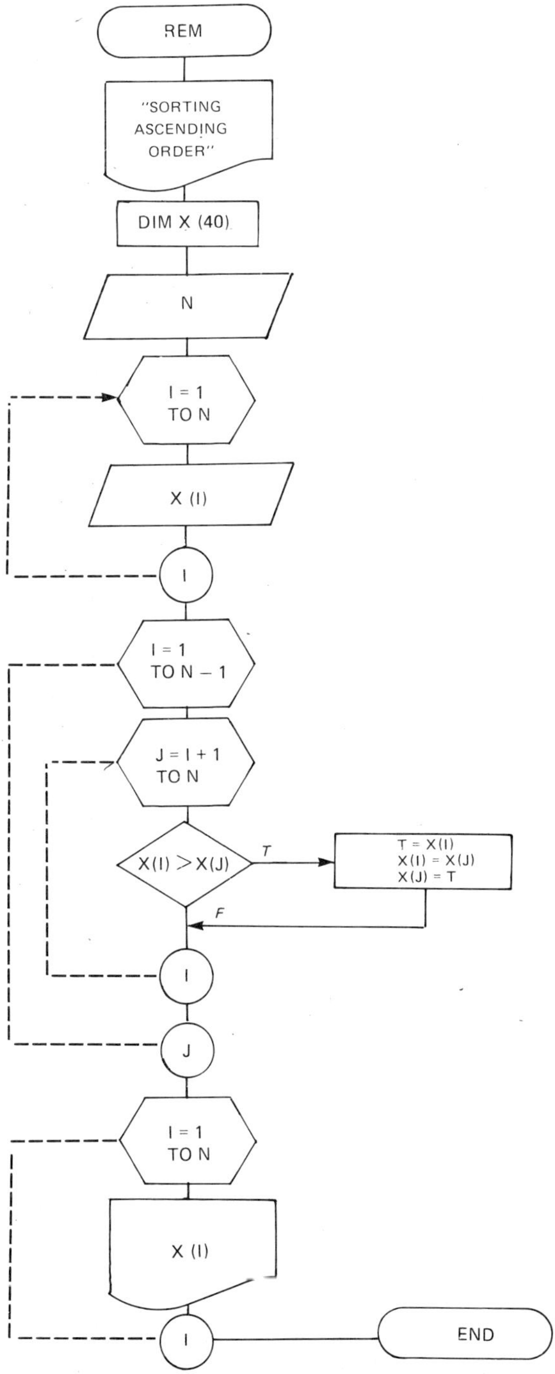
REM
"SORTING
ASCENDING
ORDER"
DIM X (40)
N
I = 1
TO N
X (I)
I
I = 1
TO N − 1
J = I + 1
TO N
X(I) > X(J)
T
T = X(I)
X(I) = X(J)
X(J) = T
F
I
J
I = 1
TO N
X (I)
I
END

Figure 6-1

6.2 Vectors and Matrices

A vector is a one-dimensional array. In mathematical notation, one defines row vectors as

$$X = (X_1, X_2, X_3)$$

or column vectors as

$$Y = \begin{pmatrix} Y_1 \\ Y_2 \\ Y_3 \\ Y_4 \end{pmatrix}$$

The subscript indicates the component of the vector to which reference is made. In a geometric interpretation, the components of the vector correspond to the coordinates of its endpoint in a Cartesian coordinate system (except for a parallel displacement).

In BASIC, subscripted variables are identified by a variable name, followed by the subscript in parentheses. Thus, the two vectors above would be written as

X(1)   X(2)   X(3)

and

Y(1)
Y(2)
Y(3)
Y(4)

A matrix is a two-dimensional array. Using matrix notations, a system of linear equations, such as

$$A_{1,1} X_1 + A_{1,2} X_2 + A_{1,3} X_3 = B_1$$
$$A_{2,1} X_1 + A_{2,2} X_2 + A_{2,3} X_3 = B_2$$
$$A_{3,1} X_1 + A_{3,2} X_2 + A_{3,3} X_3 = B_3$$

can be expressed as

$$AX = B,$$

where the matrix A contains the coefficients

$$A = \begin{pmatrix} A_{1,1} & A_{1,2} & A_{1,3} \\ A_{2,1} & A_{2,2} & A_{2,3} \\ A_{3,1} & A_{3,2} & A_{3,3} \end{pmatrix}$$

In BASIC, the elements of a matrix are identified by a variable name and two subscripts enclosed in parentheses, such as A(1,2). The first subscript indicates the row and the second indicates the column. For example, in the matrix

$$B = \begin{pmatrix} 9 & 5 \\ 3 & 6 \\ 1 & 8 \end{pmatrix}$$

B(3,1) = 1 since B(3,1) refers to the element in the third row of the first column.

Vectors in BASIC can be either numeric or string type, and the names have to be assigned accordingly. Thus, C(4) refers to the fourth component of the numeric vector C, and D$(2) refers to the second element of the string vector D$.

Matrices (or two-dimensional arrays) in BASIC can only be of the numeric type; string matrices are not permitted.

It was mentioned in chapter 2 that a memory location is assigned to each variable name as it is first encountered; later references to the same variable name will apply to the same location.

For a vector or matrix, a number of locations are required. The information that a variable name will be used for an array and the size of the array are established in a dimension statement. This statement has the general form

n DIM ⟨array name (dimension), array name (dimension). . .⟩

where n is the statement number, array name is the variable name that will be used in the program for the vector or matrix, and dimension is the maximum value the subscript(s) can assume. For example

```
20  DIM  X(2),  B(3),  A(3,2)
```

specifies that X and B are vectors and A is a matrix; X has two elements, B has 3 elements, and A has 3 rows and 2 columns.

The DIM statement is a nonexecutable statement. Its only effect is that memory locations will be set aside at the beginning of program execution. These will typically be initialized to 0 until other values are assigned through input or assignment statements.

If no dimensions are specified, a default range from 0 to 10 will be assumed for each subscript. It is absolutely necessary to give a DIM statement for larger arrays. It is advisable for small arrays to conserve storage area. For example, for the statement

```
20 DIM X(2), B(3), A(3,2)
```

a total of 14 (3 + 4 + 7) locations will be allocated. The default allocation would be 143 (11 + 11 + 11 × 11).

Subscripts can be constants, variables, or arithmetic expressions. Expressions will be evaluated and truncated to an integer. It is not permissible to use a subscripted variable as a subscript. Care should be taken that the subscript value does not become negative or exceed the maximum given in the DIM statement; otherwise, an error message will be given and program execution will stop.

6.3 Reading, Storing, and Printing of Vectors and Matrices

Vectors and matrices can be read in a loop. This is simple in the case of the vector; figure 6-2 contains a program segment that will read a vector.

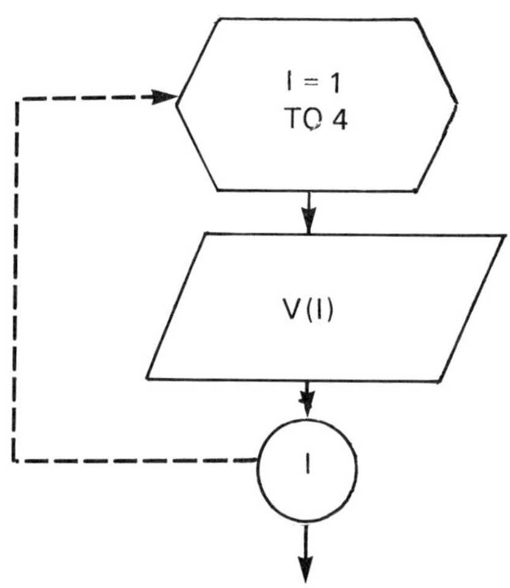


```
60 FOR I = 1 TO 4
70 READ V(I)
80 NEXT I
```

Figure 6-2

To read a matrix, a set of nested loops is required. Two-dimensional arrays in BASIC are stored by rows; therefore, the loops have to be arranged in such a manner that the second subscript varies most rapidly. Figure 6-3 shows a program segment to read a 2 by 4 matrix W and also shows how the elements of the matrix will be stored.

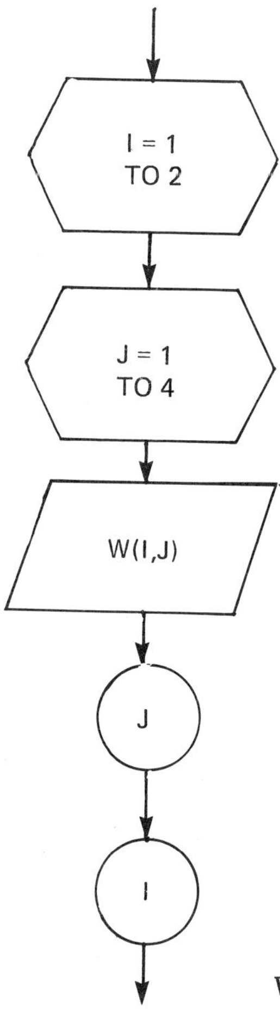


```
100  FOR I = 1 TO 2
110  FOR J = 1 TO 4
120  READ W(I,J)
130  NEXT J
140  NEXT I
```

STORAGE

$W_{1,1}$ $W_{1,2}$ $W_{1,3}$ $W_{1,4}$ $W_{2,1}$ $W_{2,2}$ $W_{2,3}$ $W_{2,4}$

Figure 6-3

To print a vector or matrix, similar principles apply. The simplest case of printing a column vector is shown in figure 6-4. In this case, one value will be printed in each line.

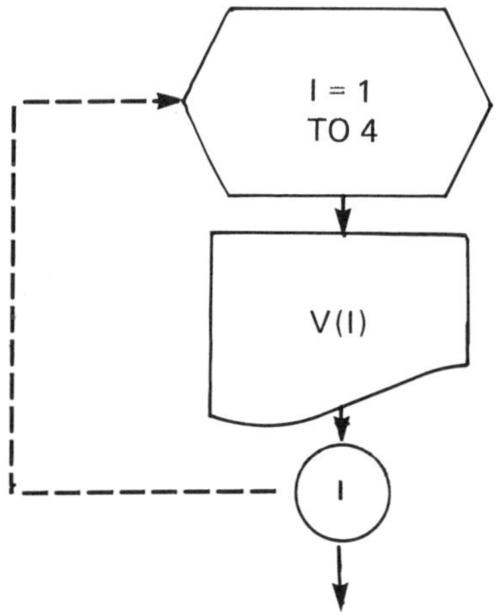


```
160  FOR I = 1 TO 4
170  PRINT V(I)
180  NEXT I
```

Figure 6-4

It is also possible to print the one-dimensional array as a row vector, provided the number of elements is not too large for one line. This is accomplished by simply adding a semicolon to the PRINT statement, as follows

```
260  FOR I = 1 TO 4
270  PRINT V(I);
280  NEXT I
```

Printing a matrix requires a little more thought. If a PRINT statement such as statement 170 in figure 6-4 is used, the matrix is printed as a column vector, i.e., the elements are printed one to a line without regard to their row and column in the matrix. If a semicolon is added to the PRINT statement, as many elements as will fit will be printed in a row, with the remainder in the second and following rows. This requires less paper, but still does not show the arrangement of the elements in the matrix. In figure 6-5, a program segment is given that illustrates how a matrix can be printed. The PRINT statement in line 240 causes the next row of the matrix to be printed in a new line.

The principles discussed in this section are illustrated in the pro-

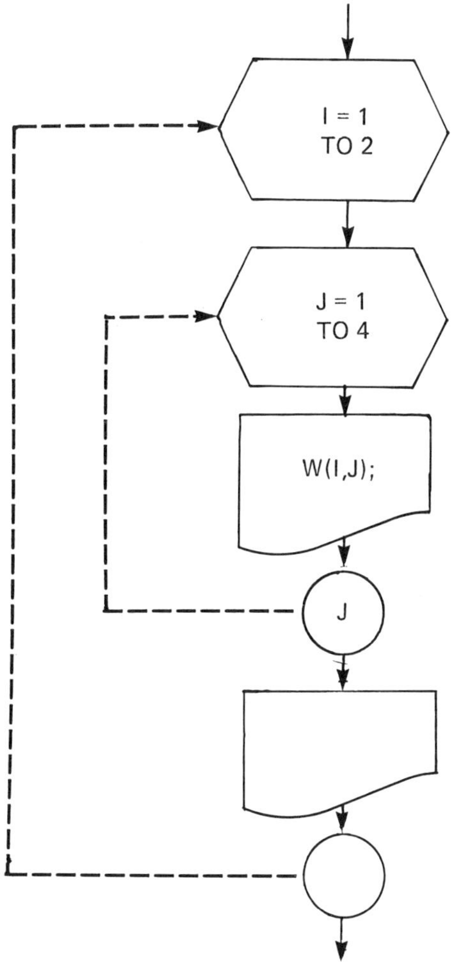


```
200 FOR I = 1 TO 2
210 FOR J = 1 TO 4
220 PRINT W(I,J);
230 NEXT J
240 PRINT
250 NEXT I
```

Figure 6-5

gram in figure 6-6. The program reads and prints the vector

$$V = (1, -1, 3, 0)$$

and the matrix

$$W = \begin{pmatrix} 2 & 0 & 1 & -3 \\ 3 & -1 & 2 & 5 \end{pmatrix}$$

```
10 REM THIS PROGRAM IS TO SHOW INPUT/OUTPUT OF ARRAYS
30 DIM V(4),W(2,4)
40 PRINT "READ A VECTOR V OF 4 ELEMENTS"
50 FOR I=1 TO 4
60 READ V(I)
70 NEXT I
80 PRINT "READ A 2 BY 4 MATRIX W"
90 FOR R = 1 TO 2
100 FOR C = 1 TO 4
110 READ W(R,C)
120 NEXT C
130 NEXT R
140 PRINT
150 PRINT "PRINT THE VECTOR V"
160 PRINT
170 FOR I = 1 TO 4
180 PRINT TAB(7);V(I)
190 NEXT I
200 PRINT
210 PRINT "PRINT THE MATRIX W"
220 PRINT
230 FOR R=1 TO 2
240 FOR C=1 TO 4
250 PRINT W(R,C);
260 NEXT C
270 PRINT
280 NEXT R
290 DATA 1,-1,3,0
300 DATA 2,0,1,-3
310 DATA 3,-1,2,5
320 END

Ready
RUN

ARRAY.IO       10:35



READ A VECTOR V OF 4 ELEMENTS
READ A 2 BY 4 MATRIX W

PRINT THE VECTOR V

        1
       -1
        3
        0

PRINT THE MATRIX W

 2  0  1 -3
 3 -1  2  5
```

Figure 6-6

6.4 Examples

With the information presented so far in chapter 6, it is possible to write programs that use subscripted variables. Three problems are illustrated in this section: the sort program described in the introduction, numerical integration using the trapezoidal rule, and multiplication of a matrix and a vector.

6.4.1 Sort Program

The principles of the bubble sort are explained in section 6.1, and a flowchart is given in figure 6-1. The reader may want to go back and review these before studying the sort program which is given in figure 6-7. It may be worthwhile to point out one detail of the program. Exchanging two values requires a temporary storage location, which is named T in the program. If X(J) were moved directly to X(I) by a LET statement

```
130  LET X(I) = X(J)
```

the value originally in X(I) would be lost, and no exchange could take place.

The DIM statement specifies a maximum subscript of 40. In the example, the array has only six elements, but the program could also be used for larger arrays and no changes (except for the two DATA statements) would be necessary. Frequently, it is not known at the time a program is written how many values will actually be processed in future applications.

6.4.2 The Area Under the Curve

Let g(x) be a continuous function on the interval [a,b]. The area under the curve can be found as

$$\int_a^b g(x)\,dx$$

where the indefinite integral, i.e., a function f(x) such that

$$\frac{df(x)}{dx} = g(x)$$

is known.

The definite integral exists even if such a function f(x) is not known. The area under the curve can be computed using a numerical approximation method such as the trapezoidal rule.

```
10 REM THIS IS A BUBBLE SORT PROGRAM
20 PRINT "SORT IN ASCENDING ORDER"
30 DIM X(40)
40 READ N
50 FOR I = 1 TO N
60 READ X(I)
70 NEXT I
80 FOR I = 1 TO N-1
90 FOR J = I+1 TO N
100 IF X(I) > X(J) THEN 120
110 GOTO 150
120 LET T = X(I)
130 LET X(I)=X(J)
140 LET X(J)= T
150 NEXT J
160 NEXT I
170 FOR I = 1 TO N
180 PRINT X(I)
190 NEXT I
200 DATA 6
210 DATA 23,54,21,54,97,56
220 END

Ready
RUN

BKEXER.P61     10:37



SORT IN ASCENDING ORDER
 21
 23
 54
 54
 56
 97
```

Figure 6-7

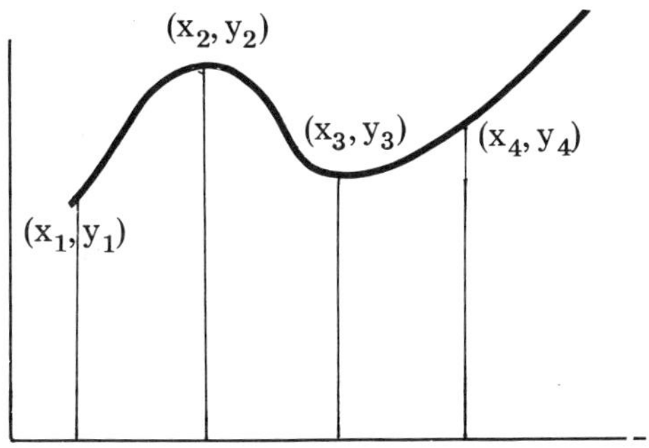

Figure 6-8

To understand the trapezoidal rule, consider figure 6-8. The interval [a,b] is divided into n equal intervals (three in figure 6-8). In each subinterval, the area under the curve is approximated by the area of a trapezoid with the endpoints X_i, X_{i+1}, $g(X_i)$ $g(X_{i+1})$. The total area under the curve is then approximated by the sum of the areas of the trapezoids. To increase accuracy of the approximation, one increases the number of trapezoids or, equivalently, decreases the length of the intervals on the x-axis.

The formulas to be used are

$$d = \frac{b - a}{n} \qquad d = \text{interval length} \quad n = \text{number of trapezoids}$$

$$x_i = a + id \qquad x_n = b, \; x_0 = a$$

$$a_i = \frac{d(g(x_{i-1}) + g(x_i))}{2} \qquad \text{area of trapezoid}$$

$$A = \sum_{i=1}^{n} a_i = \frac{d}{2} \sum_{i=1}^{n} (g(x_{i-1}) + g(x_i)) = \frac{b - a}{2n} \sum_{i=1}^{n} (g(x_{i-1}) + g(x_i))$$

The procedure to find the area under the curve involves the following steps:

1. Given a, b, and n—determine d.
2. Determine the x_i and $g(x_i)$ for $i = 0, 1, \ldots, n$.
3. Compute the area of each trapezoid and add the areas of all trapezoids.

It is not necessary to use subscripted variables for this problem, but it simplifies the logic of the program to do so. Figures 6-9 and 6-10 show the flowchart and program to compute the area under $g(x) = x^2 + 1$ in the interval [0,1].

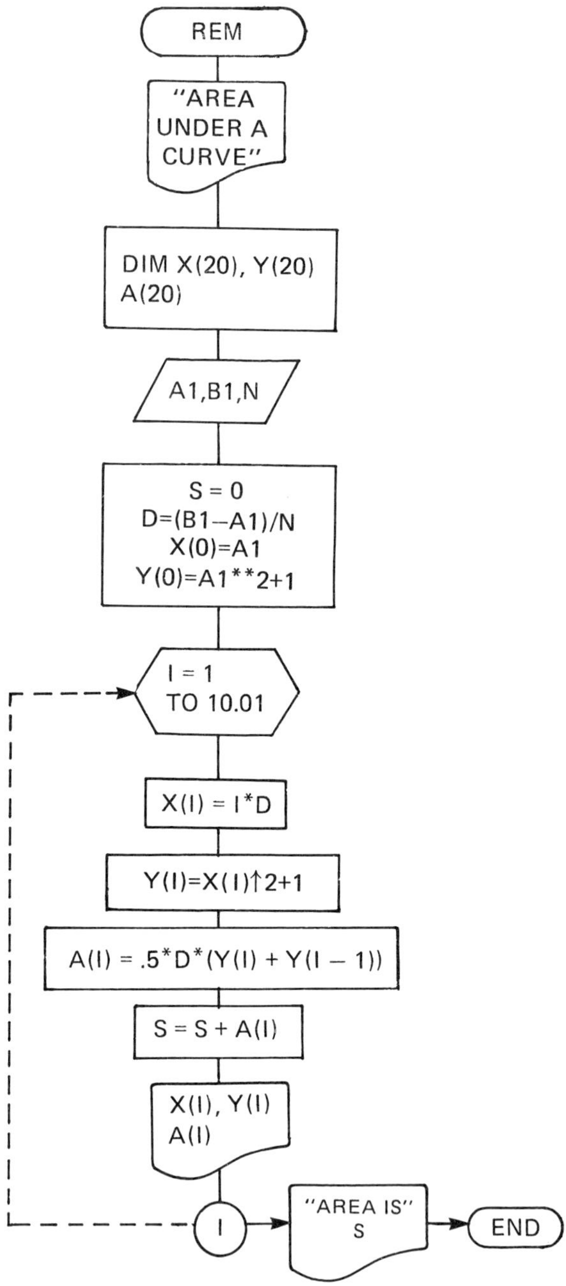
REM
"AREA
UNDER A
CURVE"
DIM X(20), Y(20)
A(20)
A1,B1,N
S = 0
D=(B1–A1)/N
X(0)=A1
Y(0)=A1**2+1
I = 1
TO 10.01
X(I) = I*D
Y(I)=X(I)↑2+1
A(I) = .5*D*(Y(I) + Y(I – 1))
S = S + A(I)
X(I), Y(I)
A(I)
I
"AREA IS"
S
END

Figure 6-9

```
10 REM FIND THE AREA UNDER A CURVE
20 PRINT "THE AREA UNDER A CURVE"
30       PRINT " THE FUNCTION IS: F(X)=X^2+1"
40       PRINT
50       PRINT "X(I)","Y(I)","A(I)"
60       DIM X(20),Y(20),A(20)
70       S=0
80       READ A1,B1,N
90       DATA 0,1,10
100      D=(B1-A1)/N
110      X(0)=A1
120      Y(0)=A1**2+1
130      FOR I=1 TO N
140      X(I)=I*D
150      Y(I)=X(I)^2+1
160      A(I)=.5*D*(Y(I)+Y(I-1))
170      S=S+A(I)
180      PRINT X(I),Y(I),A(I)
190      NEXT I
200      PRINT
210      PRINT "THE AREA IS APPROXIMATED AS ";S
220      END

Ready
RUN

AREA.3          10:40

THE AREA UNDER A CURVE
 THE FUNCTION IS: F(X)=X^2+1

X(I)            Y(I)            A(I)
 0.1             1.01            0.1005
 0.2             1.04            0.1025
 0.3             1.09            0.1065
 0.4             1.16            0.1125
 0.5             1.25            0.1205
 0.6             1.36            0.1305
 0.7             1.49            0.1425
 0.8             1.64            0.1565
 0.9             1.81            0.1725
 1               2               0.1905

THE AREA IS APPROXIMATED AS  1.335
```

Figure 6-10

Note that X(0) and Y(0) are defined as the starting point in this program. This is done before the loop; all the remaining points can be treated identically; therefore, a loop is appropriate.

The value of the integral is 1⅓. The approximation with 10 intervals is quite good. When the number of intervals is doubled (n = 20), the area is computed as 1.33375.

6.4.3 Multiplying a Vector and a Matrix

A number of problems require the multiplication of a vector and a matrix or, more generally, of two matrices. Matrix multiplication is possible if and only if the number of columns of the first matrix equals the number of rows of the second matrix. For example, it is possible to multiply

$$A = \begin{pmatrix} 9 & 5 \\ 3 & 6 \\ 1 & 8 \end{pmatrix} \qquad \text{by } X = \begin{pmatrix} 4 \\ 3 \end{pmatrix}$$

since A has two columns and X has two rows. It would not be possible to multiply X by A, in this order, since X has one column and A has three rows. Matrix multiplication is not commutative; scalar multiplication is.

The elements of the product P of two matrices A and B are computed using the formula

$$P_{ij} = \sum_{k=1}^{m} A_{ik} B_{kj}$$

A program to compute B = AX with

$$A = \begin{pmatrix} 9 & 5 \\ 3 & 6 \\ 1 & 8 \end{pmatrix} \qquad X = \begin{pmatrix} 4 \\ 3 \end{pmatrix}$$

is shown in figure 6-11. Note that the elements of A are entered by columns and those of X by row. The program is straightforward.

```
20 DIM X(2),B(3),A(3,2)
30 FOR I=1 TO 2
31 READ X(I)
32 FOR J = 1 TO 3
33 READ A(J,I)
40 NEXT J
41 NEXT I
50 FOR I = 1 TO 3
60 B(I) = 0
70 FOR J = 1 TO 2
80 B(I)=B(I) + A(I,J)*X(J)
90 NEXT J
100 NEXT I
110 PRINT "PRODUCT VECTOR B"
120 FOR I = 1 TO 3
130 PRINT B(I),
140 NEXT I
150 DATA 4,9,3,1,3,5,6,8
160 END

Ready
RUNNH


PRODUCT VECTOR B
 51            30            28
```

Figure 6-11

6.5 MAT Statements for Matrix Manipulation

Operations such as input of a matrix or multiplication of two matrices always require at least five statements since a double loop is necessary. Most versions of BASIC provide a set of matrix manipulation statements called the MAT statements which simplify the programming of matrix operations considerably. The available MAT statements and their functions are listed in table 6-1.

Table 6-1
Available MAT Statements

MAT Statement	Function
MAT READ A,B	Reads data file into elements of matrices A,B row by row — first all of A, then all of B
MAT PRINT A,B	Prints the matrices A and B by rows
MAT C = A	Assigns elements of A to corresponding elements of C
MAT C = A + B	Adds elements of B to corresponding elements of A and assigns the sums to the elements of C
MAT C = A − B	Subtracts elements of B from corresponding elements of A and assigns the results to the elements of C

MAT C = A * B	Multiplies matrix A by matrix B and assigns the products to matrix C (matrix multiplication as explained in the text)
MAT C = (k) * A	Multiplies all elements of A by k, a scalar (constant or variable) and assigns the results to the matrix C
MAT C = ZER	Assigns zeros to all elements of C
MAT C = CON	Assigns ones to all elements of C
MAT C = ION	Assigns ones to the diagonal elements of C and zeros to all other elements
MAT C = INV(A)	Assigns the inverse of matrix A to matrix C (A must be a square matrix)
MAT C = TRN(A)	Assigns transpose of matrix A to matrix C

With these statements, programs like that shown in figure 6-11 can be simplified considerably. However, for some systems the vectors X and B need to be specified as matrices (i.e., have two subscripts) so that the matrix commands can be used. For example, the vector

$$X = \begin{pmatrix} 4 \\ 3 \end{pmatrix}$$

would ordinarily be dimensioned as

DIM X(2)

However, when X is to be treated as a matrix, the dimension statement would be changed to

DIM X(2,1)

which makes X a matrix with two rows and one column — a column vector.

Figure 6-12 has examples of most of the MAT statements in table 6-1. Note that the DEC10 does not require a vector to be dimensioned as a matrix for the MAT operators to work; the vector X is used in statement 100 in a matrix multiplication. The results of the program in figure 6-12 are shown in figure 6-13.

6.6 Example: System of Linear Equations

A good illustration of the simplicity of using MAT operations is the program to solve a system of simultaneous linear equations. In chapter 4, a program was presented to solve two linear equations in

```
10 REM VECTORS AND MATRICES COMPUTATION
20 DIM X(2),Y(2),A(2,2),B(2,2)
30 DIM W(2),D(2),A1(2,2),B1(2,2),P(2),I(2,2)
40 MAT READ X,Y,A,B
50 MAT W=X+Y
60 MAT D=Y-X
70 MAT A1=INV(A)
80 MAT I=A*A1
90 MAT B1=TRN(B)
100 MAT P=A*X
110 DATA 2,6
120 DATA 8,6
130 DATA 2,1,3,5
140 DATA 6,4,5,3
150 PRINT "VECTOR X"
160 MAT PRINT X
170 PRINT "VECTOR Y"
180 MAT PRINT Y
190 PRINT "MATRIX A"
200 MAT PRINT A
210 PRINT "MATRIX B"
220 MAT PRINT B
230 PRINT "SUM OF X + Y"
240 MAT PRINT W
250 PRINT "THE DIFFERENCE OF Y-X"
260 MAT PRINT D
270 PRINT "THE INVERSE OF A"
280 MAT PRINT A1
290 PRINT "THE PRODUCT OF A AND ITS INVERSE"
300 MAT PRINT I
310 PRINT "THE TRANSPOSE OF B"
320 MAT PRINT B1
330 PRINT "THE PRODUCT OF A*X"
340 MAT PRINT P
350 END
```

Figure 6-12

two unknowns (see figure 4-13). The problem can be extended to n linear equations in n unknowns by using matrix notation. If A is the coefficient matrix, X the vector of unknowns, and B a vector of constants, the system of equations can be written as

$$\mathbf{AX} = \mathbf{B}$$

where A is a n x n matrix and X and B have n elements each.

If A is not a singular matrix, i.e., Det A $\neq$ 0, the equation can be solved by

$$X = A^{-1} B$$

where A^{-1} is the left inverse of A, or

$A^{-1} A = I$ I = identity matrix

```
VECTOR X


 2
 6


VECTOR Y


 8
 6


MATRIX A


 2              1

 3              5
```

```
MATRIX B

 6              4

 5              3

SUM OF X + Y

 10
 12

THE DIFFERENCE OF Y-X

 6
 0

THE INVERSE OF A

 0.714286      -0.142857

-0.428571       0.285714

THE PRODUCT OF A AND ITS INVERSE

 1.             0

 0              1.

THE TRANSPOSE OF B

 6              5

 4              3

THE PRODUCT OF A*X

 10
 36
```

Figure 6-13

Using MAT operations, the program to solve a system of linear equations is so simple that a flowchart is not necessary. The program and results for a system of equations such as

$$3\,x_1 + 4\,x_2 + x_3 = 4$$
$$x_1 + 4\,x_2 - 2\,x_3 = 0$$
$$2\,x_1 + x_2 + x_3 = 1$$

are given in figure 6-14.

```
10 REM USE THE MATRIX OPERATION STATEMENTS
20 PRINT "USE MATRIX OPERATION STATEMENTS "
30 PRINT "TO SOLVE SET OF SIMULTANEOUS EQUATIONS"
40  PRINT "IN THE MATRIX NOTAION AS: A * X = B"
50 PRINT "A1 IS THE INVER. OF A "
60 DIM A(3,3), X(3,1), B(3,1), A1(3,3)
70 PRINT
80 MAT READ B
90 MAT READ A
100 MAT A1=INV(A)
110 MAT X=A1*B
120 PRINT "MATRIX A"
130 MAT PRINT A
140 PRINT
150 PRINT "VECTOR B"
160 MAT PRINT B
170 PRINT "VECTOR X"
180 MAT PRINT X
190 DATA 4,0,1
200 DATA 3,4,1
210 DATA 1,4,-2
220 DATA 2,1,1
230 END
```

```
USE MATRIX OPERATION STATEMENTS
TO SOLVE SET OF SIMULTANEOUS EQUATIONS
IN THE MATRIX NOTAION AS: A * X = B
A1 IS THE INVER. OF A

MATRIX A


 3              4              1

 1              4             -2

 2              1              1

VECTOR B


 4

 0

 1

VECTOR X


-1.33333

 1.44444

 2.22222
```

Figure 6-14

For large n, this is not the ideal way to solve the system of equations; iterative methods are often more accurate than matrix inversion. However, the given solution is conceptually the simplest.

If the matrix is singular or close to it, i.e., the determinant is almost 0, the following message

% singular matrix inverted in line n

is printed out. Values are stored in the matrix for the inverse, A^{-1}; however, A^{-1} A does not equal I for that inverse. The user needs to check whether a matrix is singular before using the INV function or ignore the results after the error message is printed.

EXERCISES

1. Consider the following program

```
 10 DIM X(10)
 20 READ N
 30 DATA 8,4,2,6,10,8,12,9,3
 40 FOR I = 1 TO N
 50 READ X(I)
 60 NEXT I
 70 LET L = X(1)
 80 FOR J = 1 TO N
 90 IF X(J) <= L THEN 110
100 LET L = X(J)
110 NEXT J
120 PRINT L
130 END
```

a. What is the objective of the program?
b. How many elements (subscripted variables) are in the array X?
c. Will the program run if the J's in statement 80 through 110 are changed to I's?
d. Will the result remain the same if statement 70 is changed to

```
70 LET L = X(N)
```

e. What value will be stored in X(4) before the second loop (statement 80-110) is started?
f. What value will be stored in X(4) after the second loop is done? (Answer in terms of the original problem.)
g. What value will be printed?

2. Consider the following program

```
 10 DIM Y(4,5)
 20 READ M,N
 30 DATA 3,4,4,5,3,6,4,7,9,8,4,3,2,8
 35 LET S = 0
 40 FOR I = 1 TO M
 50 FOR J = 1 TO N
 60 READ Y(I,J)
 70 LET S = S + Y(I,J)
 80 NEXT J
 90 NEXT I
100 PRINT S
110 LET R2 = 0
120 FOR J = 1 TO N
130 LET R2 = R2 + Y(2,J)
140 NEXT J
150 PRINT R2
160 END
```

   a. What does S represent?
   b. What does R2 represent?
   c. What will the program print out?
   d. Will the program run if statements 80 and 90 are interchanged?
   e. What is the value stored in Y(2,3)?

3. Use one-dimensional arrays X, Y, and Z to write program segments to do the following exercises.
   a. To specify arrays X, Y, and Z of 5 subscripted variables (elements) each.
   b. To set all subscripted variables of the array Z equal to zero. (Use the FOR-NEXT loop).

4. Assume that the values of X and Y are

X	Y
4	9
3	6
2	5
5	3
8	4

Z is an array with values equal to the square of the difference of X and Y such that

$$Z_i = (X_i - Y_i)^2$$

Write a program segment to read the values for X and Y, calculate Z and print the output in three vertical columns titled X, Y, and Z.

5. Refer to exercise 4 and assume that the array Z has been calculated and stored. Write a program segment to find the sum of the elements of Z, called S.

6. Use all the information available from the previous exercises, that is

X	*Y*	*Z*
4	9	25
3	6	9
2	5	9
5	3	4
8	4	16

Write a program segment to find the average of the X values and call it M.

Programming Problems

1. Write a program that reads in an array of 5 numbers such as 2, 4, 6, 7, and 9, and print it twice: once as a row vector: 2, 4, 6, 7, 9, and once as a column vector:

   2
   4
   6
   7
   9

2. Provide a program to convert the mileage chart to a distance chart in metric system. Use your own data.

3. Given the observed frequency and the expected frequency as O_i and E_i respectively, construct a program to calculate the value of the chi-square, X^2, statistic for goodness of fit test as:

$$X^2 = \sum_{i=1}^{n} \frac{(O_i - E_i)^2}{E_i}$$

This X^2 statistic will measure the closeness of the agreement between the observed frequencies and expected frequencies. Use the sample data as:

O_i = 10,48,45,52,6,12,14

E_i = 11.6,46.5,49.25,50.6,9.2,10.5,12

4. Let X be an array of 10 numbers. Write a program to calculate and store the mean, the variance, and the standard deviation of the numbers of X in M,V, and S respectively. These parameters can be defined as:

$$M = \sum_{i=1}^{n} X_i/n, \ V = \sum_{i=1}^{n} (x_i - M)^2/n, S = \sqrt{V}$$

where n = number of values in X.
Use the sample data as: 3, 1, 2, 5, 4, 2, 3, 4, 6, and 8.

5. Use nested loops to solve the following problem:
   a. Read the data from the table below into a 3 by 2 array A:

4	3
6	4
9	7

   b. Print the array A as shown in the table.
   c. Find and print the transpose of array A and name it T.
   d. Multiply A and T and store the results in P.
6. Construct a program to read in a mileage chart for 10 cities. For example M(3,6) presents the distance between the 3rd and the 6th cities which is equal to M(6,3). The program will also print the chart neatly. Use real data by selecting 10 big cities near the city where you live.
7. Suppose B is a (3 × 3) symmetric matrix [i.e., B(2,3) = B(3,2)]. In this case the elements above the diagonal are equal to the elements below the diagonal. Construct a program to print only the elements below the diagonal. Use any data appropriate for this problem.
8. Given matrices A, B, and C as:

$$A = \begin{bmatrix} 1 & 2 & 5 \\ 6 & 1 & 8 \end{bmatrix} \quad B = \begin{bmatrix} 4 \\ 7 \end{bmatrix} \quad C = \begin{bmatrix} 2 & 5 & 3 \\ 3 & 2 & 7 \\ 4 & 6 & 8 \end{bmatrix}$$

   a. Provide a DIM statement for A, B, C as described above.
   b. Write a program segment for reading data into these matrices, A, B, and C.

c. Provide a DIM statement for matrix D which will be the product matrix of A and C.
d. Calculate matrix D which is equal to the product of A and C.
e. Find the transpose of matrix C and name it C1.
f. Find the inverse of matrix C and call it C2.

9. Consider the following equations:

$$2x + y + z = 4$$
$$x + 3y + 2z = 3$$
$$3x + 4y + 7z = 3$$

Let $A = \begin{bmatrix} 2 & 1 & 1 \\ 1 & 3 & 2 \\ 3 & 4 & 7 \end{bmatrix}$ and $B = \begin{bmatrix} 4 \\ 3 \\ 3 \end{bmatrix}$

Find the solution Vector $V = \begin{bmatrix} x \\ y \\ z \end{bmatrix}$

Note: $V = A^{-1}B$

10. Construct a program that does the matrix column interchange. Assume that A is square matrix as:

$$A = \begin{bmatrix} 2 & 5 & 8 & 3 \\ 3 & 7 & 5 & 6 \\ 5 & 6 & 4 & 2 \\ 4 & 2 & 3 & 5 \end{bmatrix}$$

First, read the data into the matrix X using a MAT statement. Then manipulate the column interchange to form matrix Y in which the second and the third columns of X are interchanged. Finally, print the resulting matrix, Y.

7

Expanded Input/Output Operations

7.1 Introduction

BASIC has very simple input/output features which are sufficient for many applications. However, the fixed output format is not always convenient, especially when tables are to be printed which might require more than five items per line. Also, use of the READ and DATA statement requires a program change every time a new set of data is to be used. This is awkward if the input values depend on the results of a previous run. Actually, BASIC can handle more complex input/output operations, and these will be discussed in this chapter.

By way of introduction, let us consider two problems that require more sophisticated input/output statements. In chapter 5.4, Newton's method for finding roots of equations was illustrated. To use this method, a starting value x had to be found. This can be done graphically. To draw the graph, values of the function must be found. For functions that are not polynomials this would probably involve the use of a computer or a calculator. It would be desirable to have the computer do the computations and plot the function, thus eliminating the manual steps in the process. With expanded output statements, it is possible to do just that. In section 7.2 we will explain the statements needed to write a plot program, and an example will be given in section 7.4.

Since a plot will only cover a limited interval of the independent variable, it is necessary to specify the endpoints of the interval to be used. If one has very little idea a priori where the roots will be, it may be necessary to plot first over a large interval (which means a plot that is not very detailed since we are limited to 72 characters) and then pick smaller intervals to find a better approximation. It would be desirable to specify the interval at execution time rather than change the program for each new trial. In section 7.3, we will show how data can be input at execution time.

7.2 Extensions of the PRINT Statement

The PRINT statement, as we have discussed it so far, has two features that are not always desirable: (1) items are printed in fixed print zones of 14 or 15 characters each, (2) all information is left-justified. This leads to printouts such as the table of e^x and e^{-x} shown in figure 7-1.

7.2.1 Spacing

The spacing on the print line can be controlled in three ways: by using a comma (,), a semicolon (;), or the TAB function. We are already familiar with the comma and semicolon; both were explained in chapter 2.

The TAB function allows the user to determine the exact print position in which the next item will be printed. The TAB function has the format

TAB <expression>

where expression can be an integer, a real number, or an arithmetic expression. The argument of the TAB function will always be truncated to an integer. On the DEC-10, the first print position is position 0.[1] Therefore, a TAB (1) will cause a printing in the second print position. Figure 7-2 illustrates the use of the TAB function.

Note:

1. The X in the title line is the fourth character on the line; since the first character is counted as print position 0, a TAB (3) causes a printing in the fourth character position.
2. The numbers under X are printed in the fourth postition with a TAB (2) (the 2.4 is truncated to 2); since numeric fields are printed with a sign position, each positive number is preceded by a blank so that printing of the numeric field has actually started in print position 2 as indicated by the TAB function.

---

[1]This may vary from system to system; please check your system's manual.

```
10 PRINT " X", " EXP(X)"," EXP(-X)"
15 PRINT
20 FOR I = 1 TO 10
30 LET Y1 = EXP(I)
40 LET Y2 = EXP(-I)
50 PRINT I,Y1,Y2
60 NEXT I
70 END

Ready
RUN

EXPO            11:23


 X              EXP(X)          EXP(-X)

 1              2.71828         0.367879
 2              7.38906         0.135335
 3              20.0855         4.97871E-2
 4              54.5981         1.83156E-2
 5              148.413         6.73795E-3
 6              403.429         2.47875E-3
 7              1096.63         9.11882E-4
 8              2980.96         3.35463E-4
 9              8103.08         1.23410E-4
 10             22026.5         4.53999E-5
```

Figure 7-1

3. The TAB (6) and TAB (16) for the title and TAB (5) and TAB (15) for the numeric values for EXP (X) and EXP (−X) work the same way as explained under 1 and 2.
4. For X = 10, the value of EXP (X) (22026.5) starts in position 7 instead of 6. Since a number is always printed with a trailing blank and a sign position, two positive numbers are always separated by two blanks and this rule overrides the TAB function.
5. The TAB (15) in statement 50 is preceded by a comma. This

causes an advance to the next print zone before the TAB is evaluated. For X = 1 through X = 9, the value of EXP (X) ends in print position 12 (character 13); the comma implies a move to print position 14, and the TAB then causes a move to position 15 as expected.

For X = 10, however, the value of EXP(X) ends in print position 13 (for reasons explained previously); the entire first print zone is taken up. Therefore, the comma causes the skipping of the second print zone, and the 4.53999E−5 is printed in the third print zone. The TAB (15) has no effect once the printout has passed position 15.

6. In the last line, the words IT and END are printed without a separator. Since print position 6 has been passed when the IT is reached, the TAB (6) has no effect. String variables are printed as shown in the PRINT statement, without preceding or trailing blanks; thus, the END is attached directly to the IT. (Compare with X = 10 to see the difference in handling numeric and string variables.)

```
10 PRINT TAB(3) "X";TAB(6)"EXP(X)";TAB(16)"EXP(-X)"
20 FOR I = 1 TO 10
30 LET Y1 = EXP(I)
40 LET Y2 = EXP(-I)
50 PRINT TAB(2.4) I;TAB(5.8)Y1,TAB(15) Y2
60 NEXT I
70 PRINT TAB(3) "THIS IS IT";TAB(6) "END"
80 END

Ready
RUN

TABF            19:42


    X  EXP(X)      EXP(-X)
    1  2.71828     0.367879
    2  7.38906     0.135335
    3  20.0855     4.97871E-2
    4  54.5981     1.83156E-2
    5  148.413     6.73795E-3
    6  403.429     2.47875E-3
    7  1096.63     9.11882E-4
    8  2980.96     3.35463E-4
    9  8103.08     1.23410E-4
    10  22026.5                     4.53999E-5
    THIS IS ITEND
```

Figure 7-2

To summarize, the following rules govern the spacing of printout within a line:

1. A comma in the list of a PRINT statement causes the carriage to move to the first print position of the next print zone; this holds true also if the carriage is at the beginning of a print zone, i.e., that print zone will be skipped.
2. A semicolon will suppress the move to the next print zone.
3. A numeric item will be printed in the form

   S ⟨nnn⟩ b

   where S is the sign position (blank for positive, – for negative), n indicates a digit, and b is a trailing blank; as many digits as required will be printed.
4. A string item will be printed as shown in the PRINT statement; no leading or trailing blanks will be added.
5. TAB (n) will cause the item following the TAB function to be printed in print position n. If n is not an integer, it will be truncated to an integer. Values for n can be between 0 and 71. If the current print position is greater than n, the TAB function will be ignored.

7.2.2 PRINT USING and Image Statements

As figure 7.2 illustrates, even with the TAB function it is not possible to print tables in the way we would usually prefer to see them, with decimal points lined up and numbers right justified. To do that in BASIC, two statements are available, the PRINT USING and image statements.

The PRINT USING statement has the form

n_1 PRINT USING n_2,<list>

where n_1 is the statement number of the PRINT USING statement and n_2 is the statement number of the image statement; list is a list of constants and variables (as in the PRINT statement). The list has to contain at least one item, which was not the case with the simple print. Each PRINT USING statement[1] is accompanied by an image statement which has the form:

n : <image specifications>

where n is the statement number and : is the "keyword" for the image statement. Following the colon the desired format of the output line is described; each character following the colon corresponds to one character on the printline. The available image specifications are

[1]The image statement can be incorporated into the PRINT USING statement, as will be discussed later.

#	numerical format (each # represents one digit or the sign position)
.	decimal point
blank	skip one position in the print line for each blank in the image statement.
↑	to be used with exponential format
'	indicates the beginning of a format for string variables
L,R,E	are used to describe the positioning of string variables in a field

All other characters — or the characters listed previously if they are not recognized as parts of a numeric or string format — will be printed out as they appear in the image statement. These image specifications are illustrated in figure 7-3 and 7-4 and are discussed later.

Image specifications for the printing of numeric data are used to indicate the expected size of the number in the printline. Figure 7-3 illustrates these specifications in statement 80. This statement provides for three numbers to be printed on the line, the first in print positions 1-3 (remember, the first position is position 0), the second in positions 6-14, and the last in positions 17-26. With the PRINT USING statement, numbers are right-justified in these fields as can be seen in figure 7-3.

The image for I provides for three characters even though we know that there will be at most two digits. This is done because BASIC always requires a sign position for numeric data. Thus, the smallest numeric specification is ##, describing a one-digit number. An image specification of # would be printed out as # and not be recognized as a numeric image.

The decimal point in the image specification indicates where the decimal point should be in the printout. In the second specification in statement 80, there are two # signs following the decimal point. The printout shows that e^x is printed out with two decimal places, and the decimal points are lined up.

The up-arrows (↑ or ∧) in the image statement indicate that the number should be printed in exponential format. This format was explained in detail in chapter 2. Note that two # signs are required in front of the decimal point (to provide for the sign) and 4 up-arrows must be used for the exponent. If, for example, only 3 up-arrows are used, the number will be printed in regular form and 3 up-arrows will be printed (3.456↑↑↑).

Some additional comments on numeric formats:

— If the format specification is too small, the number will still be

```
5 LET A$ = "EXP(X)"
10 PRINT USING 20, "X","EXP(X)","EXP(-X)"
20 :  'R   'CCCCCCC   'LLLLLLL
30 FOR I = 1 TO 10
40 LET Y1 = EXP(I)
50 LET Y2 = EXP(-I)
60 PRINT USING 80, I, Y1, Y2
70 NEXT I
80 : ###  ######.##  ##.###^^^^
90 END

Ready
RUN

PRNT.US         14:34


    X      EXP(X)      EXP(-X)
    1        2.72      3.679E-01
    2        7.39      1.353E-01
    3       20.09      4.979E-02
    4       54.60      1.832E-02
    5      148.41      6.738E-03
    6      403.43      2.479E-03
    7     1096.63      9.119E-04
    8     2980.96      3.355E-04
    9     8103.08      1.234E-04
   10    22026.47      4.540E-05
```

Figure 7-3

printed out, but it will be preceded by an ampersand (&), and all remaining printout in that line will be shifted to the right (see figure 7-4).
— If no decimal point is provided in the image specification, the number will be truncated before printing. Thus, 7.1, 7.5, and 7.9 will all be printed out as 7 under an image specification of *##*.
— On the other hand, for printout with decimal places, numbers are rounded; for example, 7.586 will be printed as 7.59 under an image specification of *##.##*.

Image specifications for the printing of string variables are indicated in figures 7-3 and 7-4. The image specification for a string

```
10 FOR I = 1 TO 5
20 PRINT USING 30, 10**I,I
30 : #####  ##
40 NEXT I
50 PRINT
60 LET A$="***"
70 LET M$ = "--------"
80  PRINT M$
90 PRINT USING 200,A$
100 PRINT USING 210, A$
120 PRINT USING 220, A$
130 PRINT USING 230,A$,M$
200 :'LLLLLLL
210 :'CCCCCCC
220 :'RRRRRRR
230 :'E
240 END

Ready
RUN

FIGUR4          10:35



    10   1
   100   2
  1000   3
 10000   4
 &100000   5

--------
***
  ***
     ***
***
--------
```

Figure 7-4

variable starts with an apostrophe ('); if this is left out, the letters L, C, R, E will not be recognized as image specifications and will be printed as they appear in the image statement.

An image specification of n L's causes the string variable to be left-justified in a field of n + 1 print positions (the apostrophe counts as a print position). If the string variable has m > n + 1 characters, the right-most m − (n + 1) characters will not be printed. The first line of asterisks in figure 7-4 and the heading EXP(−X) in figure 7-3 have been printed with the L specification.

An image specification of n R's causes the string variable to be right-justified in a field of n + 1 print positions (again, the apostrophe counts as a print position). If the string variable has m > n + 1 characters, the right-most m − (n + 1) characters will now be printed left-justified as described previously. The third line of asterisks in figure 7-4 and the heading X in figure 7-3 have been printed with the R specification.

An image specification of n C's causes the string variable to be centered in a field of n + 1 print positions (the apostrophe is, again, counted as a print position). If the string variable has m > n + 1 characters, the variable will be printed left-justified and the last m − (n + 1) characters will be omitted. The second line of asterisks in figure 7-4 and the heading EXP(X) in figure 7-3 have been printed with the C specification. As can be seen from figure 7-4, if it is not possible to center the string variable exactly in the field (such as centering three characters in a field of 8), the extra character will be added at the left.

An image specification of 'E causes the string variable to be printed left-justified in a field the length of which will be determined at execution time. With an E specification, the entire string variable will be printed regardless of its length; the programmer does not need prior knowledge about the maximum length of the variable. In figure 7-4, both the last line of asterisks and the last line of dashes are printed with an 'E image specification. One disadvantage of the 'E specification is that it is not possible to control where additional fields will be printed; they will always be shifted to the right based on the length of the string variable printed with the E specification.

Figure 7-4 illustrates one other characteristic of the PRINT USING and image statement: if the list in the PRINT USING statement contains more variables than the image statement contains specifications, the image statement will be used repeatedly (see statements 130 and 230 and the two last lines of the printout.)

So far, we have always used a PRINT USING and separate image statement. However, it is also possible to include the image in the

PRINT USING statement which leads to the following format

n PRINT USING<string formula, list>

where n is a statement number; string formula is the image specification, enclosed in quotation marks ("); and list is a list of items to be printed as described earlier for the PRINT and PRINT USING statement.

For example

10 PRINT USING " 'CCC ", A$

is equivalent to the two statements

10 PRINT USING 20, A$

20 : 'CCC

It is largely a matter of personal preference which form of the PRINT USING statement is used.

7.3 INPUT Statement

In chapter 2 we discussed the READ and DATA statements as a way to provide data to the program. Since the DATA statement is part of the program, a change in values always requires a change in the program. It is also possible in BASIC to provide data during the execution of the program. In that case, the INPUT statement is used. It has the format

n INPUT<variable list>

where n is a statement number and variable list contains the names of the variables for which values need to be supplied. When the INPUT statement is reached, a question mark is printed at the terminal. The user then types in the appropriate values, separated by commas and ending with a carriage return. The carriage return signals the end of the input, and program execution continues.

Figure 7-5 shows another version of the program to print a table of e^x and e^{-x}. In this case, the user can determine at execution time over which interval and in which increments the table should be printed.

```
10 PRINT "ENTER MIN X, MAX X, INCREMENT"
20 INPUT X1,X2,D
30 PRINT
40 PRINT USING 150, "X"
50 FOR I = X1 TO X2 BY D
60 LET Y1 = EXP(I)
70 LET Y2 = EXP(-I)
```

```
80 PRINT USING 160, I,Y1,Y2
90 NEXT I
100 PRINT
110 PRINT "DO YOU WANT TO CONTINUE?"
120 PRINT "TYPE Y OR N"
130 INPUT Q$
140 IF Q$ = "Y" GO TO 10
150 :    'R       EXP(X)      EXP(-X)
160 :####.##  ##.###^^^^  ##.###^^^^
170 END

Ready
RUN




ENTER MIN X, MAX X, INCREMENT
 ?1.95,2.0,.01

     X       EXP(X)       EXP(-X)
   1.95    7.029E+00    1.423E-01
   1.96    7.099E+00    1.409E-01
   1.97    7.171E+00    1.395E-01
   1.98    7.243E+00    1.381E-01
   1.99    7.316E+00    1.367E-01

DO YOU WANT TO CONTINUE?
TYPE Y OR N
 ?Y
ENTER MIN X, MAX X, INCREMENT
 ?1.95,2.005,.01

     X       EXP(X)       EXP(-X)
   1.95    7.029E+00    1.423E-01
   1.96    7.099E+00    1.409E-01
   1.97    7.171E+00    1.395E-01
   1.98    7.243E+00    1.381E-01
   1.99    7.316E+00    1.367E-01
   2.00    7.389E+00    1.353E-01

DO YOU WANT TO CONTINUE?
TYPE Y OR N
 ?N
```

Figure 7-5

Note that the INPUT statement (20) is preceded by a PRINT statement (10) with instructions for the user. This is useful to insure that the data are entered in the correct order. The INPUT statement in line 130 is likewise preceded by instructions; without these it would at times be difficult to know which information is required in response to the "?". The explanation is for the benefit of the user; BASIC does not require a PRINT statement to accompany the INPUT statement.

Statement 50 is an example of a FOR statement using increments other than 1. The table will be printed for X = X1, X1 + D, X1 + 2D, and for all values X1 + nD < X2. Since internal computations are done in binary, X2 may not be reached exactly, even if the user has set up his limits in such a manner that the maximum value should be reached. When the maximum is given as 2.0, execution stops with 1.99; an upper limit of 2.005 insures that all desired values are actually printed.

Statement 20 and 130 illustrate that the INPUT statement can be used for numeric and string variables. If the type of the input value does not correspond to the type of the variable in the INPUT statement, an error message, such as

```
?INPUT DATA NOT IN CORRECT FORM – PLEASE
RETYPE
?
```

will be printed. The user then has another chance to enter the data.

7.4 Example — Plot Program

As mentioned in sections 5.4 and 7.1, the starting value for Newton's method is usually found graphically. For all but the simplest functions, the values for the graph would probably be found using a computer, for example, by having a table such as that in figure 7-5 printed out. But it is not necessary to plot the values manually; a computer program can be used to generate plots either on the printer or on a special plotter.

Figure 7-6 shows a program in BASIC which plots $y = x - .5e^{.5x}$, the function used in section 5.4 to illustrate Newton's method. After functions and subroutines have been explained in chapter 8, it will be possible to write a general plot program which does not have a specific function built into it. The purpose of the program in figure 7-6 is to illustrate how the PRINT USING statement can be used to plot a function, not to show how to write the ideal plot program.

```
10   REM   PROGRAM TO PLOT A FUNCTION
20  REM
30  DIMENSION P(55,35),X(20),Y(20),Y3(10)
40 REM
50  REM  INITIALIZE
60  REM
90  MAT P = ZER
100  LET S$ = "*"
120  LET B$ = " "
130 FOR I = 1 TO 20
140 LET X(I) = .05*I
150 LET Y(I) = X(I) - .5*EXP(.5*X(I))
160 NEXT I
220  REM
230  REM     DETERMINING SCALES
240  REM
250 LET X1 = X2 = X(1)
260 LET Y1 = Y2 = Y(1)
310 FOR I = 2 TO 20
320  IF X(I) < X1 THEN 350
330  IF X(I) > X2 THEN 370
340  GO TO 380
350  LET X1 = X(I)
360  GO TO 380
370  LET X2 = X(I)
380  IF Y(I) < Y1 THEN 410
390  IF Y(I) > Y2 THEN 430
400  GO TO 440
410  LET Y1 = Y(I)
420  GO TO 440
430  LET Y2 = Y(I)
440  NEXT I
500  LET D1 = X2 - X1
510  LET D2 = Y2 - Y1
515  IF D1<=1 THEN 521
519  LET S1=INT(D1/3 + .5)
520  GO TO 529
521  LET S1=D1/3
522 LET C = 1
523  LET N1=INT(S1*10**C)
524  IF N1>0 THEN 528
```

```
525  LET C = C+1
526  IF C>5 THEN 620
527  GO TO 523
528  LET S1=N1/10**C
529  IF D2<=1 THEN 532
530  LET S2 = INT (D2/8 + .5)
531  GO TO 540
532  LET S2=D2/8
533 LET C=1
534  LET N2=INT(S2*10**C)
535  IF N2>0 THEN 539
536  LET C = C+1
537  IF C>5 THEN 620
538  GO TO 534
539  LET S2=N2/10**C
540  LET X3 = X1
550  LET X4 = X1 + S1
560  LET X5 = X4 + S1
570  LET X6 = X5 + S1
580  FOR I = 1 TO 10
590  LET Y3(I) = Y1 + S2*(I-1)
600  NEXT I
610  GO TO 680
620  PRINT "D1 = " D1," D2 = "D2
630  PRINT "UNDERFLOW, RUN ABORTED"
640  GO TO 2000
650  REM
660  REM        FILLING IN POINTS
670  REM
680  FOR I = 1 TO 20
684  LET T1 = (X(I) - X1)/S1
688  LET T2 = INT(T1 + .005)
692  LET I1 = 1+T2*10+INT((T1-T2)*10+.5)
696  LET T3 = (Y(I) - Y1)/S2
700  LET T4 = INT(T3 + .005)
704  LET I2 = 1+T4*6+INT((T3-T4)*6+.5)
707 IF I2 >55 GO TO 720
710  LET P(I2,I1) = 1
720  NEXT I
730  REM
740  REM          PRINTING
750  REM
760  FOR I = 55 TO 1 BY -1
765  LET A$ = "I"
770 FOR J = 1 TO 35
```

```
774  IF P(I,J) = 1 THEN 786
778  LET A$ = A$ + B$
782  GO TO 790
786  LET A$ = A$ + S$
790  NEXT J
800  LET I1 = (I-1)/6
810  IF I1 - INT(I1) > 0 THEN 830
814  PRINT USING 816,Y3(I1+1),A$
816  :####.##'LLLLLLLLLLLLLLLLLLLLLLLLLLLLLLLLLLLL
820  GO TO 850
830  PRINT USING 840, A$
840  :       'LLLLLLLLLLLLLLLLLLLLLLLLLLLLLLLLLL
850  NEXT I
852  LET M$="-+---------+---------+---------+---"
854  PRINT USING 840, M$
858  PRINT USING 860, X3, X4, X5, X6
860  :    ####.#    ####.#    ####.#    ####.#
870  GO TO 2000
2000 END
```

Figure 7-6

The plot program has four distinct parts: (1) the setting of all initial values and the data to be plotted; (2) the determination of the appropriate scale; (3) the setting up of the array to be printed; and (4) the actual printing. A general plot routine would also provide for these parts. A simpler plot program might read in the scale values and possibly even the array to be printed.

The initialization part of the program is found in statements 90 through 160. Here the characters to be used in the plot, * and blank, are defined. The matrix P will later be filled with 1's and 0's indicating where the function is to be plotted. The loop from 130 to 160 computes the values that will be used for the plot. An INPUT statement could be used to define range and increment.

The scaling part is necessary for a program that is written in fairly general terms since 72 characters, at most, are available for the plot and these could correspond to an interval from X = 0 to X = 1 or from X = 0 to X = 100, to list just two examples.

Statements 250 through 440 find the minimum and maximum values of X and Y. Statements 500 through 610 perform the actual scaling task. In this part, the interval length (maximum X − minimum

X) is divided by 3, and 1" on the plot will then correspond to

$$\frac{x_3 - x_1}{3}$$

units of X. For Y, the program provides for 8" and a correspondence of 1" of printout to $\frac{y_2 - y_1}{8}$ units of Y.

Difficulties arise when only a small interval, such as (0,1), is to be plotted. In this case, 1" corresponds to an interval of length < 1 which will make S1 = 0. Statements 522 through 528 are in the program to deal with that case. Statements 529 through 539 fulfill the same purpose for Y.

Finally, statements 540 through 600 set up the values that correspond to 1" intervals on the plot. Figure 7-7 illustrates the process.

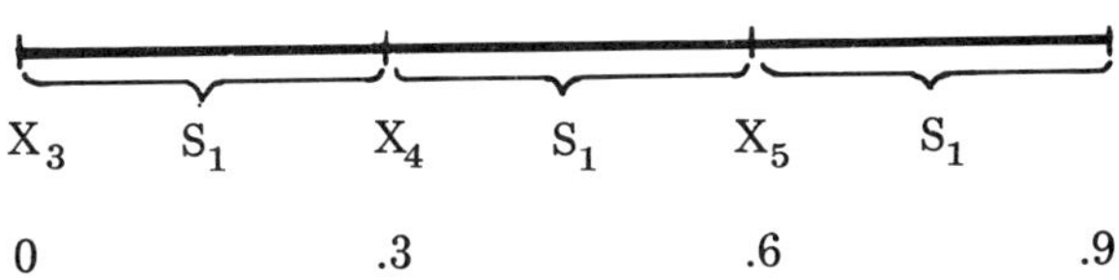

Figure 7-7

Statement 680 through 720 set up the array P which had been initialized to 0. For each point to be plotted, a 1 will be entered at the appropriate place; all other entries remain 0. The basic principle involved is to find out how far from the origin a given point is and translate that into print positions — 10 positions to an inch horizontally and 6 positions to an inch vertically. For example T2 indicates how many inches to move from the origin, and T2*10 translates that into print positions; (T1 − T2)*10 allocates print positions for the fraction of an inch exceeding T2.

The actual printing is fairly easy. The printline is stored in A$. This string is built up a character at a time. The "I" will generate the vertical axis. For each 0 in P, a blank is added; for each 1, an * will be printed and is added to A$. Note that adding string variables has the effect of linking them together.

Finally, the IF statement in 810 determines when the vertical axis should be labelled; a value will be printed every inch (every 6 lines).

The plot generated by this program is shown in figure 7-8.

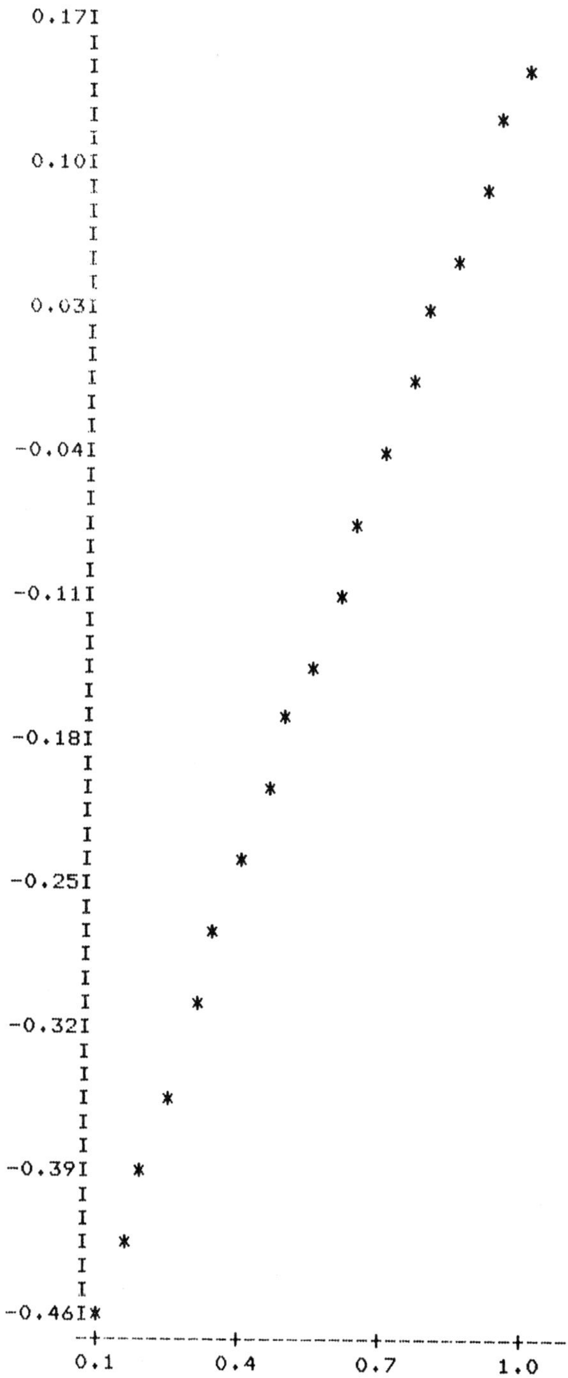

Figure 7-8

EXERCISES

1. Show the output with a precise indication of the location of the values for the following exercises, when A = 10.5, B = −2, C$ = "USA".

   a. **100 PRINT TAB(10);"START"**

   ----

   b. **110 PRINT TAB(5);A;TAB(15);B**

   ----

   c. **120 PRINT TAB(5);C$;TAB(15);B**

   ----

   d. **130 PRINT C$;TAB(10);A;B**

   ----

   e. **140 PRINT TAB(12.5);B;A**

   ----

   f. **150 PRINT "YEAR",TAB(12);1981**

   ----

2. Identify and correct the errors in the statements below:

   a. **10 PRINT "TYPE 1 FOR YES AND 2 FOR NO"**
      20 INPUT A$

   b. **30 PRINT "ENTER I.D. NUMBER AND NAME"**
      40 INPUT ID, N$

   c. **50 PRINT "ENTER THE DATE AS: DD-MM-YY"**
      60 INPUT D,M,Y

   d. **70 PRINT "ENTER THE TWO SHORTER SIDES OF A TRIANGLE"**
      80 INPUT A,B,C

3. Given

   A = 1500, B = .065, C = 1, D = −25.20,

   E$ = "UPDATED INFORMATION"

   a. Write the appropriate PRINT USING and image statements to print E$, A, and D with five spaces between E$ and A, and two spaces between A and D.

   b. Write the image statement that produced the following output

      THE UPDATED INFORMATION: B=0.065 AND C=1

      if the PRINT USING statement is as follows:

      100 PRINT USING 110, E$,B,C

Programming Problems

1. Construct a program to print a diagonal line of "*"'s across a square of 10 by 10 print positions. Use the FOR-NEXT loop and the TAB function.
2. Write an interactive program to calculate the function:

   F(X) = 1 + X + X ^ 2 + X ^ 3 + X ^ 4 + X ^ 5

   for values of X supplied at execution time.
3. Write a program to convert from Fahrenheit to Centigrade such as

   C = 5/9 (F−32)

   Enter the temperature in Fahrenheit using an INPUT statement.
4. Write a program to print the numbers from 1 to 6, with an increment of .5, the squares and the square roots of the numbers. Print the results with two decimal places, in column form, and centered under suitable headlines.

8

User-Defined Functions and Subroutines

8.1 Introduction

The built-in functions which were discussed in chapter 3 are actually subprograms — small programs which were developed at the time the BASIC compiler was created and are stored as part of the BASIC programming system. These functions were developed to perform specific tasks and can be called in any user program. The subprogram is incorporated into the user's program when the function is referenced in a statement in the program.

Built-in functions are available for commonly used operations. However, a programmer who writes a series of programs for an application may use an algorithm repeatedly which is not generally utilized, but is specific to this application. BASIC allows the user to define her own functions and subroutines which can then be referenced in the user program similar to the way built-in functions are used.

For example, the binomial probability distribution may be used in acceptance sampling. The probability of finding defectives in a sample of n items is

$$p(d) = \binom{n}{d} p^d q^{n-d}$$

where p is the probability of finding a defective in the total shipment and $q = 1 - p$. A program might be written to compute the probability of accepting a bad lot and the probability of rejecting a good lot for varying sampling plans. In this case, the binomial probability function has to be evaluated at several points in the program. It is then simpler for the programmer to define the function once and call it at several places in the program.

We will discuss how to define functions in section 8.2 and how to define subroutines in section 8.4. Some detailed examples will be given in sections 8.3 and 8.5.

8.2 User-defined Functions

In the simplest case, a user-defined function may only require one arithmetic expression. In this case, one statement is used in BASIC to define this function. This statement has the general form

n DEF FNa(variable list) = ⟨expression⟩

where n is the statement number and FNa is a three-letter function name, the first two letters of which have to be FN. The variable list contains those variables which are used in the expression on the right-hand side of the equal sign; values for these variables are supplied at the time the function is referenced in the program.

For example, a function to compute the volume of a sphere can be defined by the statement

30 DEF FNV (R) = (4/3)*3.1416*R3**

where the numerical value of the radius R will be provided at execution time.

A user-defined function can have more than one independent variable. For example, the formula for the mass of a moving body is

$$m = \frac{m_0}{\sqrt{1 - \frac{V^2}{c^2}}}$$

where M_o is the mass at rest, v is the speed of the body relative to an observer, and c is the speed of light. If this formula has to be used repeatedly in a program, a function can be defined as follows:

40 DEF FNM (MO, V, C) = MO/(SQR (1 – V↑2/C↑2))

A simple statement function can be written for any formula that fits on one line. The function may have no argument at all, but will usually have one or more. The function can be defined at any place in the program (before the END statement). Each function name may be used only once in a DEF statement, i.e., the function cannot be redefined. It is possible to use variables in the expression that are not part of the variable list; values must be assigned to these variables in the program before the function is called. A function definition can also use a previously defined function in the expression on the righthand side of the equal sign.

A user-defined function is called in the same way as a built-in function: the function name is used in an arithmetic expression, and the values for which the function is to be evaluated are listed in parentheses. For example, to compute the volume of a sphere of radius 10, one would use the statement

100 LET V = FNV (10)

where FNV is the function defined previously (statement number 30) and the value 10 will be substituted for R in the equation on the right.

The number and type of arguments in the statement that calls a function has to agree with the number and type of arguments in the DEF statements. The statements

50 DEF FNA (A, B, C) = SQR(A + B) * C
200 LET X1 = FNA (1, 2, 3, 4)

would result in the error message

? Incorrect number or type of arguments in line 200

This error is detected at execution time.

An example of a program using a statement function is given in figure 8-1. The function,

$$Y = \frac{e^x - e^{-x}}{2}$$

is defined in statement 30 and is called in statements 50 and 60.

Not all functions can be defined in one statement. For example, a function to find n! = n (n − 1)∗(n − 2). . . 2∗1 requires a loop so that at least three statements are necessary. In this case, the definition of the function takes the form

n_1 DEF FNa(variable list)
n_2 FNa = ⟨expression⟩
n_3 FNEND

where n_1, n_2, n_3 are statement numbers. The rules for naming the function and number of variables are the same as for the single-line function: names have three letters, the first two of which are FN; the variable list may be empty, as in

60 DEF FNA

but will typically contain one or more variable names. The function name has to appear at least once on the left side of an assignment statement, and the last statement has to be FNEND.

Figure 8-2 shows an example of a multiple line function. Statements 90 through 160 define a function to compute n! which is then used in statements 190, 210 and 220 to compute three factorials needed for the binomial probability computations in statement 230.

```
CH8EX.P1        10:19


10 REM THIS PROGRAM IS TO ILLUSTRATE  A STATEMENT FUNCTION
20 PRINT "THIS FUNCTION IS -- (EXP(X)-EXP(-X))/2 "
30 DEF FNS(X)=(EXP(X)-EXP(-X))/2
40 READ N
50 LET F1=FNS(N)
60 LET F2=FNS(2*N)
70 LET D=F2-F1
80 PRINT "FOR X=";N;"THE FUNCTION VALUE IS";F1
90 PRINT "FOR X=";2*N;"THE FUNCTION VAULE IS";F2
100 PRINT "THE DIFFERENCE IS"; D
110 DATA 4
200 END

Ready
RUN

CH8EX.P1        10:20


THIS FUNCTION IS -- (EXP(X)-EXP(-X))/2
FOR X= 4 THE FUNCTION VALUE IS 27.2899
FOR X= 8 THE FUNCTION VAULE IS 1490.48
THE DIFFERENCE IS 1463.19
```

Figure 8-1

Note that the function definition is in the middle of the program. At execution time, control passes from statement 80 directly to statement 180, and statements 90 through 160 are executed when the function is called in statements 190, 210 and 220.

Another example of a multiple-line function is given in figure 8-3. This function finds the smaller of two values and in the case of a tie arbitrarily returns one of the values.

Rules concerning multiple line functions are:

1. It is not permissible to define one function within another function.
2. It is not permissible to transfer control out of the range of a function.
3. The function name must be assigned a value at least once between the DEF and FNEND statements. Different values can be

```
EXBINO.CH8     10:21



10 REM PROGRAM TO ILLUSTRATE A MULTIPLE-LINE FUNCTION
20 PRINT "ACCERPTANCE SAMPLING PROBLEM"
30 PRINT
40 PRINT "SAMPLE SIZE", "  P "
50 READ N,P
60 DATA 5,.05
70 PRINT N,P
80 PRINT
90 DEF FNF(N)
100 LET F=1
110 IF N<=1 THEN 150
120 FOR K=2 TO N
130 LET F=F*K
140 NEXT K
150 LET FNF=F
160 FNEND
170 REM COMPUTATION OF BINOMIAL PROBABILITIES
180 PRINT "C=DEFECT, IN SAMPLE","P OF FINDING > C DEF."
190 LET F1=FNF(N)
200 FOR I=1 TO N
210 LET F2=FNF(I)
220 LET F3=FNF(N-I)
230 LET P=F1/(F2*F3)*P^I*(1-P)^(N-I)
240 PRINT I,,P
250 NEXT I
260 END

Ready
RUN

EXBINO.CH8     10:21



ACCERPTANCE SAMPLING PROBLEM

SAMPLE SIZE      P
 5              0.05

C=DEFECT, IN SAMPLE            P OF FINDING > C DEF.
 1                              0.203627
 2                              0.20942
 3                              5.74048E-2
 4                              5.11787E-5
 5                              3.51113E-22
```

Figure 8-2

assigned as illustrated in statements 50 and 70 of figure 8-3.

4. The last statement must be a FNEND statement. In figure 8-3, statement 60 transfers control to the FNEND statement which is the end of the function subprogram. It is not possible to return

control directly to the calling statement; the FNEND statement must always be reached in the function subprogram.

An example of a program using a user-defined function is given in section 8-3.

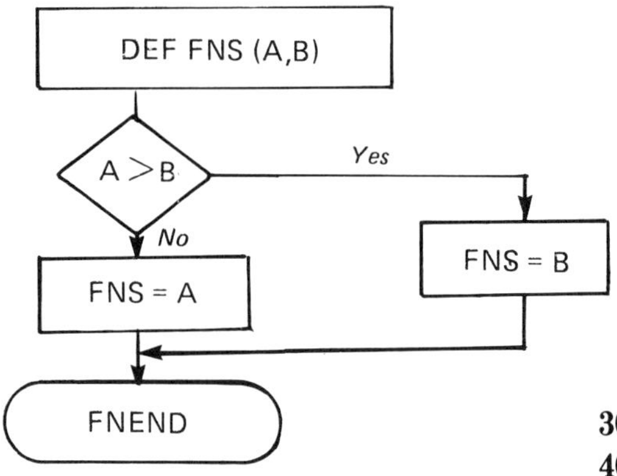


```
30 DEF FNS (A,B)
40 IF A > B THEN 70
50 LET FNS = A
60 GO TO 80
70 LET FNS = B
80 FNEND
```

Figure 8-3

8.3 Example for User-Defined Functions

In chapter 6 we discussed the trapezoidal rule to compute the area under a curve. Another approximation method is Simpson's rule.

To compute $\int_a^b f(x)\,dx$ using Simpson's rule, the interval $\{a,b\}$ is subdivided into n subintervals of width $d = \frac{b-a}{n}$ where n is an even number. In each subinterval of length 2d, such as the interval $\{x_1, x_2\}$, the function f(x) is approximated by a parabola $y = Ax^2 + Bx + C$ which passes through the midpoint and two endpoints of the interval, such as $(x_0, f(x_0))$, $(x_1, f(x_1))$, and $(x_2, f(x_2))$ in the example. Since a parabola is determined by three points, the coefficients for the parabola can be computed from the function values at the three points, and the area under the parabola can be found. For one such subinterval, the area under the parabola is

$$A_p = \frac{d}{3}\left\{ y_0 + 4y_1 + y_2 \right\}$$

Adding over all the subintervals leads to the formula

$$A_s = \frac{d}{3}(y_0 + 4y_1 + 2y_2 + 4y_3 + 2y_4 + \ldots + 2y_{n-2} + 4y_{n-1} + y_n)$$

as an approximation of the area

$$\int_a^b f(x)dx$$

where

$$y_i = f(x_i), \; d = \frac{b-a}{n}, \text{ and } x_i = a + i*d$$

Flowchart, coding, and results for a program to approximate an area by using Simpson's rule are given in figures 8-4, 8-5, and 8-6. This is an interactive program. The user specifies at execution time over which interval the integral should be evaluated and how many subintervals should be used (see statements 80, 100, and 130 in figure 8-5). The program can be rerun with different values if the user so desires — see statements 340 through 360.

Simpson's rule will not provide a correct approximation if N is an odd number. Therefore, statement 150 is used to assure an even number which is either equal to the value entered in statement 130 or one less.

The function to be evaluated is defined in statement 50. If the user wishes to use the program for a different function, only this statement has to be changed.

8.4 Subroutines

A subroutine is a self-contained program segment which can be referenced by the main program or by another subroutine within the same program. The subroutine does not have a name, and no arguments are transferred as was the case with the user-defined function. Subroutines can be used to perform complex computations or to provide input or output. Whenever a certain algorithm will be used repeatedly and in different parts of a program, it is worthwhile to define a subroutine for it.

Figure 8-7 shows the general setup of a program utilizing subroutines. The subroutines are defined in a separate part of the program (usually, but not necessarily, the end) and are called from various places in the main program.

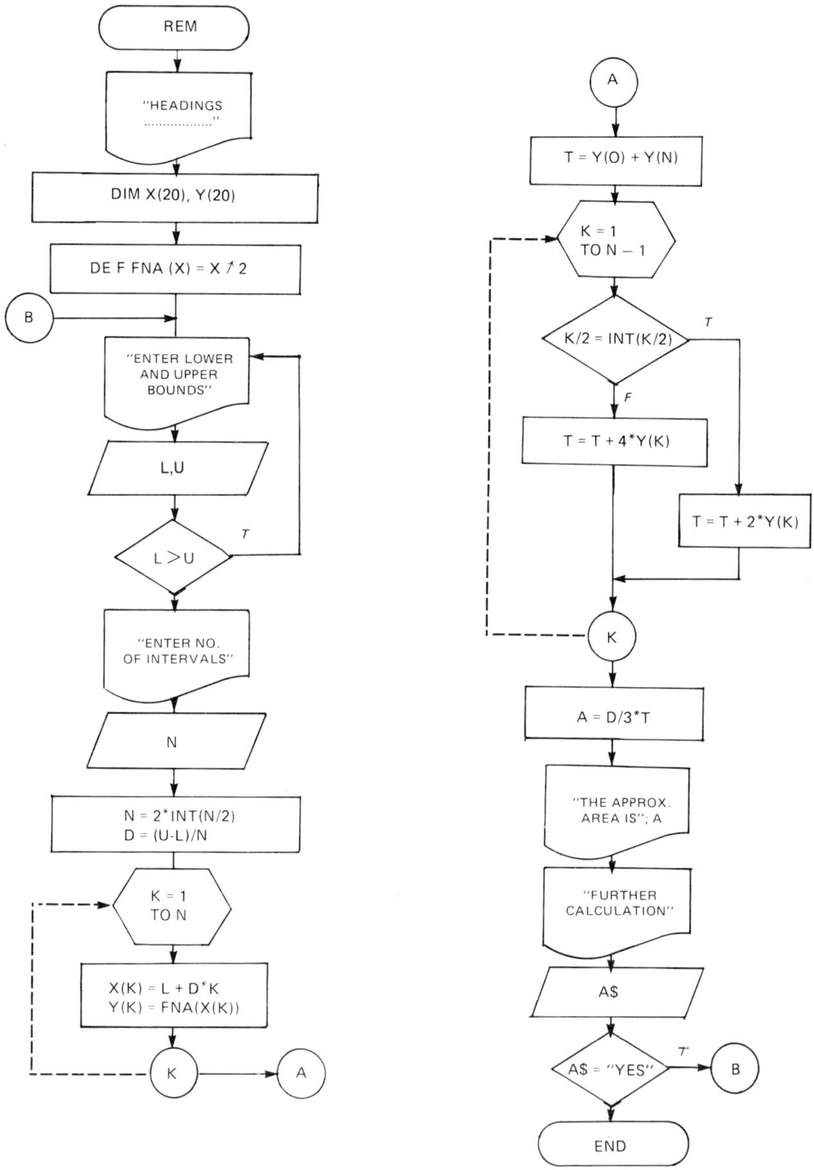
REM
"HEADINGS
................"
DIM X(20), Y(20)
DE F FNA (X) = X ↑ 2
B
"ENTER LOWER
AND UPPER
BOUNDS"
L,U
L > U
T
"ENTER NO.
OF INTERVALS"
N
N = 2*INT(N/2)
D = (U-L)/N
K = 1
TO N
X(K) = L + D*K
Y(K) = FNA(X(K))
K
A
A
T = Y(O) + Y(N)
K = 1
TO N – 1
K/2 = INT(K/2)
T
F
T = T + 4*Y(K)
T = T + 2*Y(K)
K
A = D/3*T
"THE APPROX.
AREA IS"; A
"FURTHER
CALCULATION"
A$
A$ = "YES"
T
B
END

Figure 8-4

```
REM APPROXIMATE THE AREA UNDER THE CURVE BY SIMPSON'S RULE
PRINT "APPROXIMATE THE AREA UNDER THE CURVE BY SIMPSON'S RULE"
PRINT "THE FUNCTION IS: G(X)=X^2 "
DIM X(20),Y(20)
PRINT
DEF FNA(X)=X^2
PRINT
PRINT "THE POSITIVE LOWER BOUND IS";
INPUT L
PRINT "THE POSITIVE UPPER BOUND IS";
INPUT U
IF L > U THEN 60
PRINT "NO. OF INTERVALS ( 2 TO 20)";
INPUT N
IF N < 2 THEN 120
LET N=2*INT(N/2)
PRINT
LET D=(U-L)/N
FOR K=1 TO N
LET X(K)=L+D*K
LET Y(K)=FNA(X(K))
NEXT K
LET T=Y(0)+Y(N)
FOR K=1 TO N-1
IF K/2 = INT(K/2) THEN 270
LET T=T+4*Y(K)
GOTO 280
LET T=T+2*Y(K)
NEXT K
LET A=D/3*T
PRINT
PRINT "THE AREA APPROXIMATED BY SIMPSON'S RULE IS";A
PRINT "-----------------------------------------------------------"
PRINT "ANY FURTHER CALCULATION";
INPUT A$
IF A$="YES" THEN 60
END
```

Figure 8-5

Two statements not previously discussed are necessary for the use of subroutines. The GOSUB statement "calls" the subroutine from the main program. It has the general form

$$n_1 \quad \text{GOSUB} \quad n_2$$

where n_1 is the statement number in the main program and n_2 is the number of the first statement in the subroutine.

The GOSUB statement transfers control to line n_2 and, in that way, works like a GO TO. However, it has an additional function: it "remembers" statement number n_1 and, thus, makes it possible for

```
APPROXIMATE THE AREA UNDER THE CURVE BY SIMPSON'S RULE
THE FUNCTION IS: G(X)=X^2

THE POSITIVE LOWER BOUND IS ?2
THE POSITIVE UPPER BOUND IS ?5
NO. OF INTERVALS ( 2 TO 20) ?10

THE AREA APPROXIMATED BY SIMPSON'S RULE IS 38.6
-------------------------------------------------------
ANY FURTHER CALCULATION ?YES

THE POSITIVE LOWER BOUND IS ?1
THE POSITIVE UPPER BOUND IS ?5
NO. OF INTERVALS ( 2 TO 20) ?10

THE AREA APPROXIMATED BY SIMPSON'S RULE IS 41.2
-------------------------------------------------------
ANY FURTHER CALCULATION ?NO
```

Figure 8-6

control to be returned to the main program after the subroutine has been executed. In figure 8-7, the first GOSUB statement (160) transfers control to statement 700 which is the beginning of the first subroutine. After the subroutine has been executed, the statement following the GOSUB (170) will be executed next.

The end of a subroutine is indicated by the RETURN statement. This has the general form

n RETURN

A subroutine may have more than one RETURN statement; it must contain at least one. In figure 8-7, the RETURN statement in line 890 indicates the end of the first subroutine.

Other than the RETURN, a subroutine does not contain any "special" statements. The first statement (n_2) which is referenced in the GOSUB n_2 statement can be a REM statement identifying the subroutine, or it can be the first statement needed to perform the task of the subroutine.

Figure 8-8 shows an example of a program using a subroutine. The subroutine itself is comprised of statements 210 through 260. It reverses the order of a given array. The arrays used in the subroutine, D and U, have been dimensioned in the main program (statement 30). The upper limit of the loop (N) and the values of the original array (U) have been established in the main program (statements 60 through 110). N and U are not passed to the subroutine as formal arguments; the subroutine simply refers to the memory locations defined in the main program for the same name. (Note: this differs from the way a function operates; in the function, the name is immaterial, and the argument used at execution time defines which location to go to.)

```
10      REM
        .
        .
160     GOSUB 700
170     .
        .
380     GOSUB 700
390
        .                                   MAIN PROGRAM
        .
500     GOSUB 700
510
        .
        .
560     GOSUB 900
570
600     GOTO 1000                         Control Statement
700     REM (first statement of subroutine 1)
        .
        .
        .
890     RETURN                              SUBROUTINES
900     REM (first statement of subroutine 2)
        .
        .
        .
990     RETURN
1000    END
```

Figure 8-7

The subroutine is referenced in statement 120. The GOSUB refers to the REM statement; it could also have been written as GOSUB 230 since REM statements are not executable. The RETURN statement refers control back to statement 130, the statement following the GOSUB.

Statement 200 provides a branch around the subroutine. It is always necessary to separate a subroutine from the main program by either a GO TO or a STOP statement so that the subroutine cannot be entered accidentally without a GOSUB statement. If a subroutine is entered without a GOSUB, the return address is not established and the RETURN statement cannot function properly.

In the remaining section of this chapter, we will discuss several programs that utilize functions and subroutines.

```
10 REM SAMPLE PROGRAM USING SUBROUTINE
20 PRINT "U AND D ARE ARRAYS USED IN THE PROGRAM"
30 DIM U(20),D(20)
40 PRINT "      ORIGINAL ARRAY"
50 PRINT "      -------------------"
60 READ N
70 FOR I=1 TO N
80 READ U(I)
90 PRINT USING 100, U(I)
100 :      #####
110 NEXT I
120 GOSUB 220
130 PRINT
140 PRINT "THE ARRAY IN REVERSED ORDER"
150 PRINT "-------------------------------"
160 FOR I=1 TO N
170 PRINT USING 100,D(I)
180 NEXT I
190 PRINT
200 GOTO 280
210 REM THE FOLLOWINT IS A SUBROUTINE
220 REM REVERSE THE ORDER OF A GIVEN ARRAY
230 FOR I=1 TO N
240 LET D(I)=U(N+1-I)
250 NEXT I
260 RETURN
270 DATA 5
280 DATA 23,25,45,52,58
290 END

Ready
RUN

CH8EX.P11      10:25
```

```
U AND D ARE ARRAYS USED IN THE PROGRAM
      ORIGINAL ARRAY
      --------------
          23
          25
          45
          52
          58

THE ARRAY IN REVERSED ORDER
---------------------------
          58
          52
          45
          25
          23
```

Figure 8-8

8.5 Examples

The sample problems in this section are arranged in order of increasing complexity. The last program (parking lot simulation) is a fairly realistic example of a problem for which the computer can be used to advantage. There are other programming languages which are more typically used for simulation problems; the example illustrates that it is possible to program a problem of this magnitude in BASIC.

8.5.1 Subroutines to Sort and Print

Assume that you have a number of objects which are identified by a code C. Each object has a number of characteristics, for example Q1 and Q2. It may be of interest to sort the objects on one of the characteristics in descending order and print the objects in that order. It may be determined at execution time which characteristic should be used for sorting.

The major steps in the program are

1. Read the number of objects and the data.
2. Print the original data.
3. Select the characteristics to be sorted.
4. SORT
5. Print the sorted data.

6. Decide whether to sort on another characteristic; return to three or end the program.

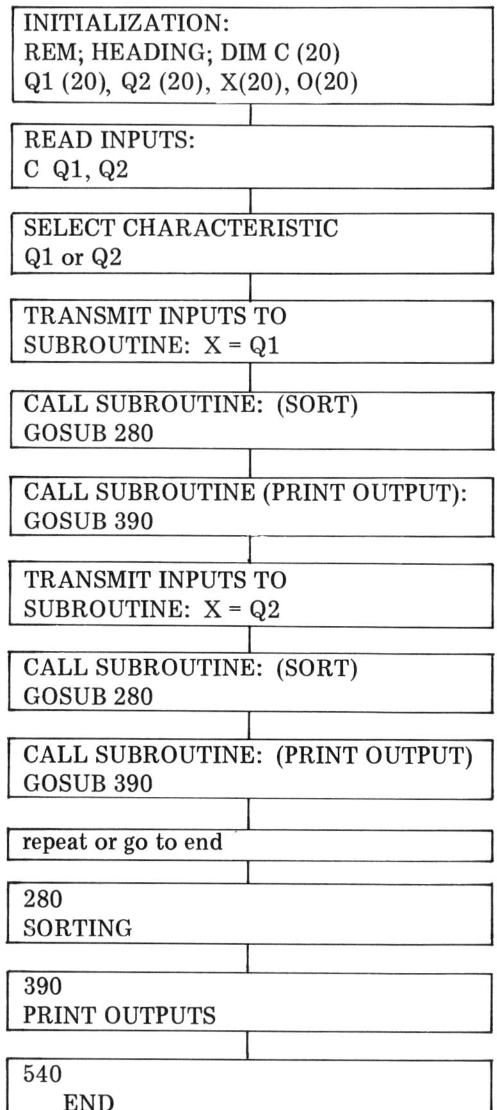

Figure 8-9

The block diagram in figure 8-9 shows the structure of the program for sorting and printing. The flowchart for the sort and the program itself are shown in figures 8-10 and 8-11. Figure 8-12 shows the results of a sample run.

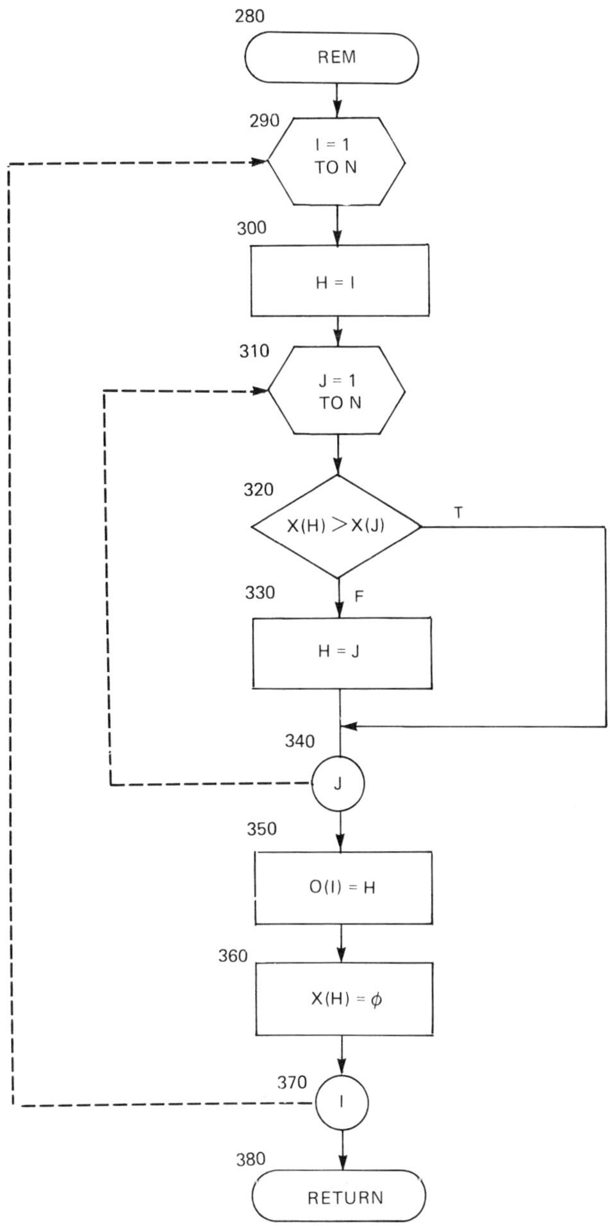
280
REM
290
I = 1
TO N
300
H = I
310
J = 1
TO N
320
X(H) > X(J)
T
F
330
H = J
340
J
350
O(I) = H
360
X(H) = ϕ
370
I
380
RETURN

Figure 8-10

```
10 REM THIS PROGRAM IS UTILIZING SUBROUTINES TO SORT AND PR
20 PRINT "DISPLAY THE DATA BASED ON THE QUALITY"
30 DIM C(20),Q1(20),Q2(20),X(20),O(20)
40 READ N
50 FOR I=1 TO N
60 READ C(I),Q1(I),Q2(I)
70 NEXT I
80 PRINT "       THE ORIGINAL VALUES"
90 PRINT "OBJECT CODE","QUALITY 1","QUALITY 2"
100 PRINT
110 FOR I=1 TO N
120 PRINT C(I),Q1(I),Q2(I)
130 NEXT I
140 PRINT "----------------------------------------------------------------"
150 PRINT "        ARRANGED BY QUALITY 1"
160 FOR I=1 TO N
170 LET X(I)=Q1(I)
180 NEXT I
190 GOSUB 280
200 GOSUB 390
210 FOR I=1 TO N
220 LET X(I)=Q2(I)
230 NEXT I
240 PRINT "       ARRANGED BY QUALITY 2"
250 GOSUB 280
260 GOSUB 390
270 GOTO 480
280 REM SUBROUTINE FOR SORTING IN DESCENDING ORDER
290 FOR I=1 TO N
300 LET H=I
310 FOR J=1 TO N
320 IF X(H)>X(J) THEN 340
330 LET H=J
340 NEXT J
350 LET O(I)=H
360 LET X(H)=0
370 NEXT I
380 RETURN
390 REM SUBROUTINE FOR PRINT OUTS
400 PRINT "OBJECT CODE","QUALITY 1","QUALITY 2"
410 PRINT
420 FOR I=1 TO N
430 LET J=O(I)
440 PRINT C(J),Q1(J),Q2(J)
450 NEXT I
460 PRINT "----------------------------------------------------------------"
470 RETURN
480 DATA 5
490 DATA 101,32,12
500 DATA 202,45,26
510 DATA 215,48,34
520 DATA 312,20,15
530 DATA 413,56,20
540 END
```

read inputs (lines 40–70)

print out the inputs (lines 110–130)

transmit the inputs to the subroutine (lines 160–180)

reference to subroutines (lines 190–200)

Figure 8-11

The sort procedure used here is not the bubble sort described in chapter 4. The sort routine works with one array, X. However, every time two elements of X are switched, it would be necessary to switch also the codes and the characteristics which are not used in the sort to keep the records intact. Rather than do that the subroutine stores the subscripts in the array O in such a way that the first subscript refers to the largest element etc. (statement 350). The subscripts in O are then used in the PRINT subroutine (see statements 430 and 440 in figure 8-11.)

```
DISPLAY THE DATA BASED ON THE QUALITY
     THE ORIGINAL VALUES
OBJECT CODE    QUALITY 1      QUALITY 2

 101             32             12
 202             45             26
 215             48             34
 312             20             15
 413             56             20
-------------------------------------
        ARRANGED BY QUALITY 1
OBJECT CODE    QUALITY 1      QUALITY 2

 413             56             20
 215             48             34
 202             45             26
 101             32             12
 312             20             15
-------------------------------------
       ARRANGED BY QUALITY 2
OBJECT CODE    QUALITY 1      QUALITY 2

 215             48             34
 202             45             26
 413             56             20
 312             20             15
 101             32             12
-------------------------------------
```

Figure 8-12

8.5.2 Program Utilizing Both Function and Subroutine

Consider the problem of finding the maximum of a function g(x) over an interval { *a,b* }. This problem can be solved analytically by solving g'(x) = 0 and checking if g''(x) < 0 for the roots of g'(x) = 0. However, it may not be possible to solve g'(x) = 0 exactly, or the roots may not be in the interval { *a,b.*}

A simple approximation would be to subdivide the interval {a,b} and compute the function value g(x) at the beginning of each subinterval. These values can be compared and the maximum can be found for this set of values.

Figure 8-13 shows a program to find the maximum for $g(x) = x^4 - 5x^3 + 7x + 2$. The output for a sample run is given in figure 8-14.

The function is defined in statement 50. If the user wishes to find the maximum for a different function, only statement 50 needs to be changed.

```
10 REM THIS PROGRAM UTILIZES BOTH DEFINED FUNCTION AND SUBROUTIN
20 PRINT "UTILIZATION OF DEFINED FUNCTION AND SUBROUTINE"
30 PRINT "    THE FUNCTION IS :G(X)=X^4-5*X^3+7*X+2"
40 PRINT
50 DEF FNF(X)=X^4 - 5*X^3 + 7*X +2
60 READ A,B,N
70 IF N=0 THEN 340
75 PRINT "-------------------------------------------------------------"
80 GOSUB 140
90 PRINT "WHEN INCREASE THE NO. OF INTERVAL BY 10"
100 PRINT
110 LET N=N*10
120 GOSUB 140
130 GOTO 60
140 REM SUBROUTINE PROCESS
150 LET D=(B-A)/N
160 PRINT "THE INTERVAL IS [";A;",";B;"]"
170 PRINT "THE DISTANCE OF EACH SUBINTERVAL IS ";D
180 LET L=A
190 LET M=FNF(A)
200 FOR X=A TO B BY D
210 IF FNF(X)<=M THEN 240
220 LET L=X
230 LET M=FNF(X)
240 NEXT X
250 PRINT
260 PRINT "MAX VALUE IS A =";M
270 PRINT "IT OCCURS NEAR X=";L
280 PRINT "-------------------------------------------------------------"
290 PRINT
300 RETURN
310 DATA 0,3,30
320 DATA 0,3,10
330 DATA 0,0,0
340 END
```

Figure 8-13

```
UTILIZATION OF DEFINED FUNCTION AND SUBROUTINE
   THE FUNCTION IS :G(X)=X^4-5*X^3+7*X+2

 --------------------------------------------------
 THE INTERVAL IS [ 0 , 3 ]
 THE DISTANCE OF EACH SUBINTERVAL IS  0.1

 MAX VALUE IS A = 5.4496
 IT OCCURS NEAR X= 0.8
 --------------------------------------------------

 WHEN INCREASE THE NO. OF INTERVAL BY 10

 THE INTERVAL IS [ 0 , 3 ]
 THE DISTANCE OF EACH SUBINTERVAL IS  0.01

 MAX VALUE IS A = 5.45887
 IT OCCURS NEAR X= 0.77
 --------------------------------------------------
--------------------------------------------------
THE INTERVAL IS [ 0 , 3 ]
THE DISTANCE OF EACH SUBINTERVAL IS  0.3

MAX VALUE IS A = 5.3111
IT OCCURS NEAR X= 0.9
--------------------------------------------------

WHEN INCREASE THE NO. OF INTERVAL BY 10

THE INTERVAL IS [ 0 , 3 ]
THE DISTANCE OF EACH SUBINTERVAL IS  0.03

MAX VALUE IS A = 5.45739
IT OCCURS NEAR X= 0.78
--------------------------------------------------
```

Figure 8-14

The subroutine to find the maximum is contained in statements 140 through 300. It is executed twice, once for N subintervals (call in statement 80) and then for 10 * N subintervals (call in statement 120). The reason for increasing the number of intervals like this is to show how stable the procedure is; as can be seen in the output in figure 8-13, there may be variations in x and g(x) for different interval sizes. Depending on the desired accuracy, the program may have to be rerun with a larger N.

8.5.3 Parking Lot Simulation [1]

Consider a company parking lot which is used by sales people. They come in at various times during the day and stay sometimes for an hour, sometimes for the entire day. On some days they do not come in at all. A simulation is needed to determine whether 20 parking spaces are sufficient for 25 drivers.

To simulate parking lot occupation, certain frequency distributions have to be available. Let us assume that all the necessary data have been collected. It is known that, on the average day, 8% of the drivers do not come in (no-show). The distribution of arrival times is given in table 8-1. The length of stay in the parking lot depends on ar-

Table 8-1
Distribution of Arrival Times

Time	Relative Frequency
7:30 - 7:59	.13
8:00 - 8:29	.10
8:30 - 8:59	.17
9:00 - 9:29	.13
9:30 - 9:59	.06
10:00 - 10:29	.035
10:30 - 10:59	.05
11:00 - 11:29	.025
11:30 - 11:59	.03
12:00 - 12:29	.015
12:30 - 12:59	.045
1:00 - 1:29	.11
1:30 - 1:59	.03
2:00 - 2:29	.02
2:30 - 2:59	.015
3:00 - 3:29	.015
3:30 - 3:59	.02

[1] The idea for this example came from Edward V. Krick, *An Introduction to Engineering and Engineering Design,* Second Edition, John Wiley & Sons.

rival time T_a and on the average follows the function $y = 10.2 - .56$ (T_a). However, there are random fluctuations in length of stay which follow the distribution given in table 8-2. With this information, a program can be written to simulate parking lot information.

Table 8-2
Deviations from Average Length of Stay

Deviation	Relative Frequency
−2.2	.008
−1.3	.056
−0.8	.112
−0.3	.250
0.0	.076
0.3	.298
0.8	.136
1.3	.056
1.6	.008

The general outline of the program is given in the flowchart in figure 8-15. The program simulates 100 days (see loop on K) and prints out only summary statistics at the end (daily averages). The printout is shown in figure 8-18. These are only some of the statistics that could be computed to aid in decision-making.

The subroutines to determine show and no-show, arrival time, and length of stay make use of the relative frequency distributions given in table 8-1 (arrival time) and 8.2 (deviation from linear function) and of the fact that 8% do not show on a given day. Arrival and departure time are determined for each of the 25 drivers (see loop on I). Then the "parking lot is filled," i.e., the elements of a matrix representing 20 parking slots and 24 half-hour time intervals are set to one if the parking space is occupied at the time; the elements are zero otherwise.

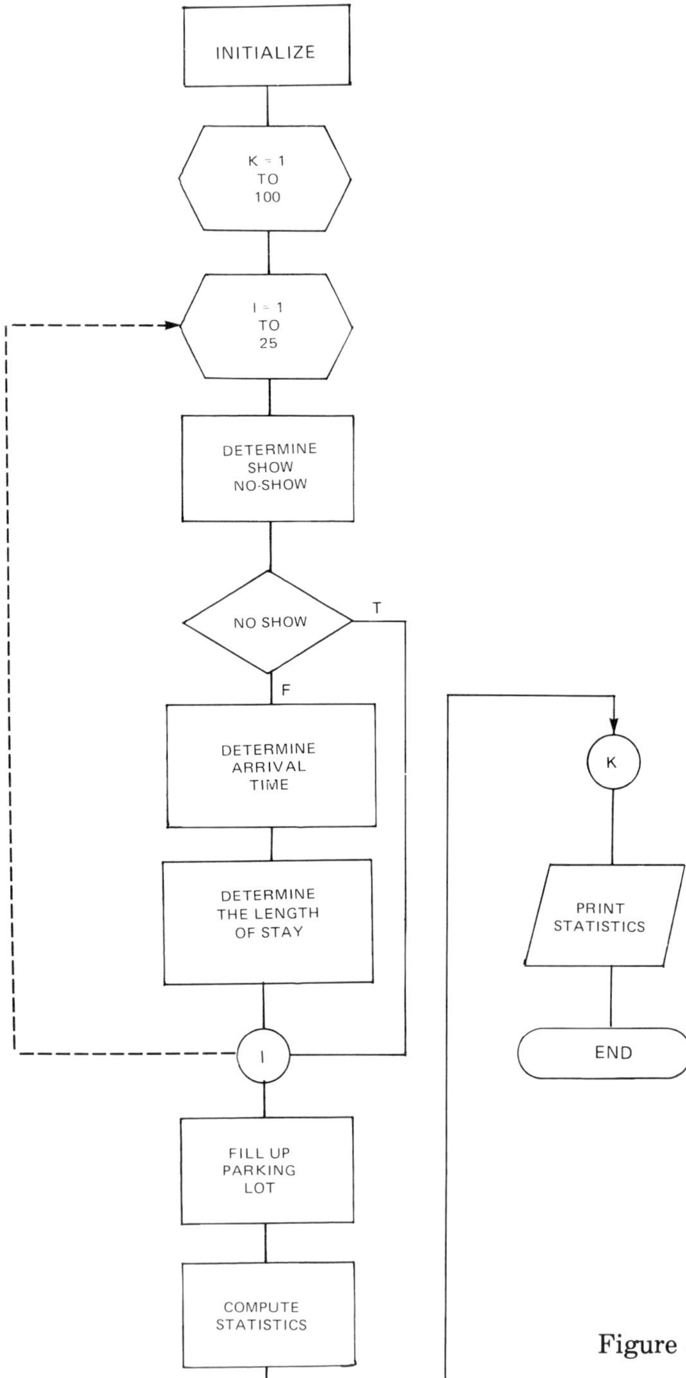
INITIALIZE
K = 1
TO
100
I = 1
TO
25
DETERMINE
SHOW
NO-SHOW
NO SHOW
T
F
DETERMINE
ARRIVAL
TIME
DETERMINE
THE LENGTH
OF STAY
I
FILL UP
PARKING
LOT
COMPUTE
STATISTICS
K
PRINT
STATISTICS
END

Figure 8-15

More detailed flowcharts for individual subroutines are given in figure 8-16. The program itself is shown in figure 8-17, and figure 8-18 represents the output from a simulation run.

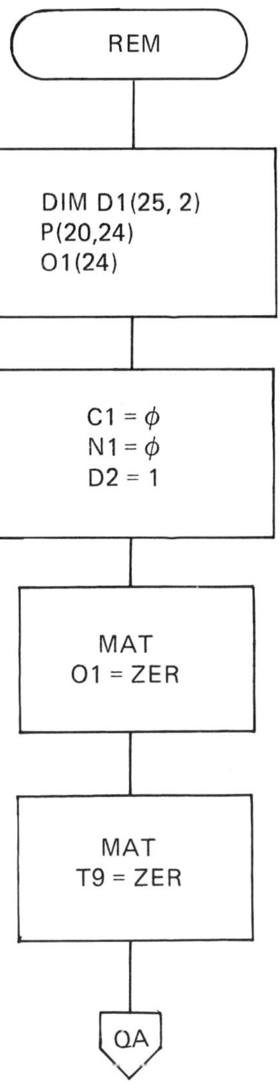

Figure 8-16

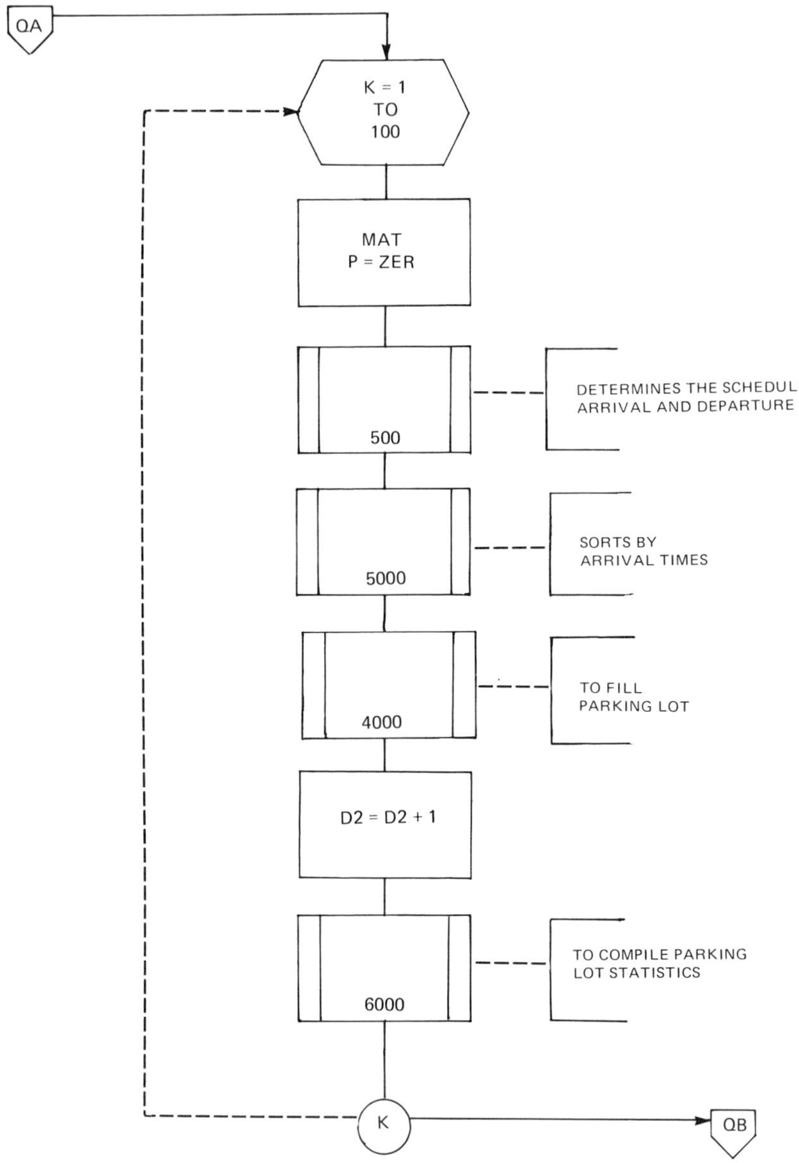
QA
K = 1
TO
100
MAT
P = ZER
500
DETERMINES THE SCHEDULE
ARRIVAL AND DEPARTURE
5000
SORTS BY
ARRIVAL TIMES
4000
TO FILL
PARKING LOT
D2 = D2 + 1
6000
TO COMPILE PARKING
LOT STATISTICS
K
QB

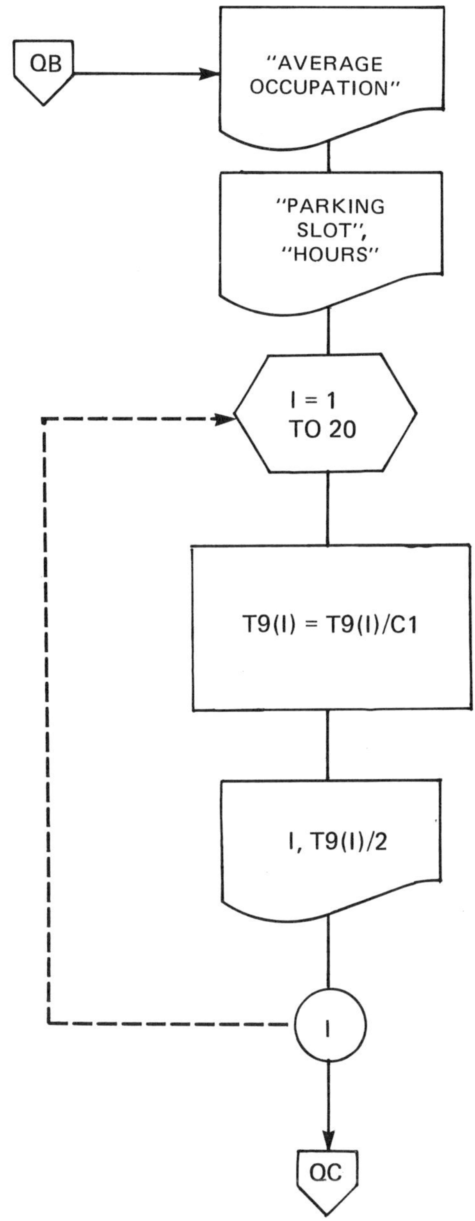

QB
"AVERAGE OCCUPATION"
"PARKING SLOT",
"HOURS"
I = 1
TO 20
T9(I) = T9(I)/C1
I, T9(I)/2
I
QC

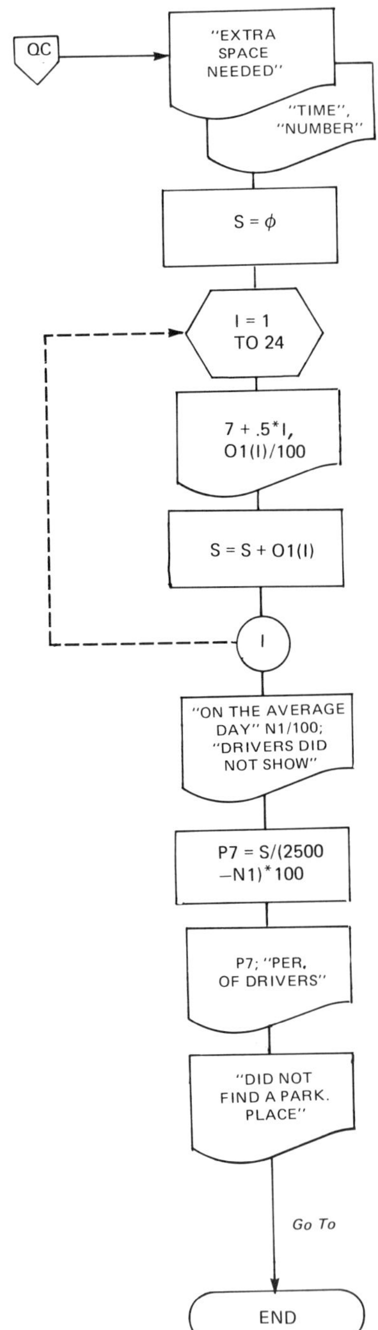
QC
"EXTRA SPACE NEEDED"
"TIME", "NUMBER"
S = ϕ
I = 1 TO 24
7 + .5*I, O1(I)/100
S = S + O1(I)
I
"ON THE AVERAGE DAY" N1/100; "DRIVERS DID NOT SHOW"
P7 = S/(2500 –N1)*100
P7; "PER. OF DRIVERS"
"DID NOT FIND A PARK. PLACE"
Go To
END

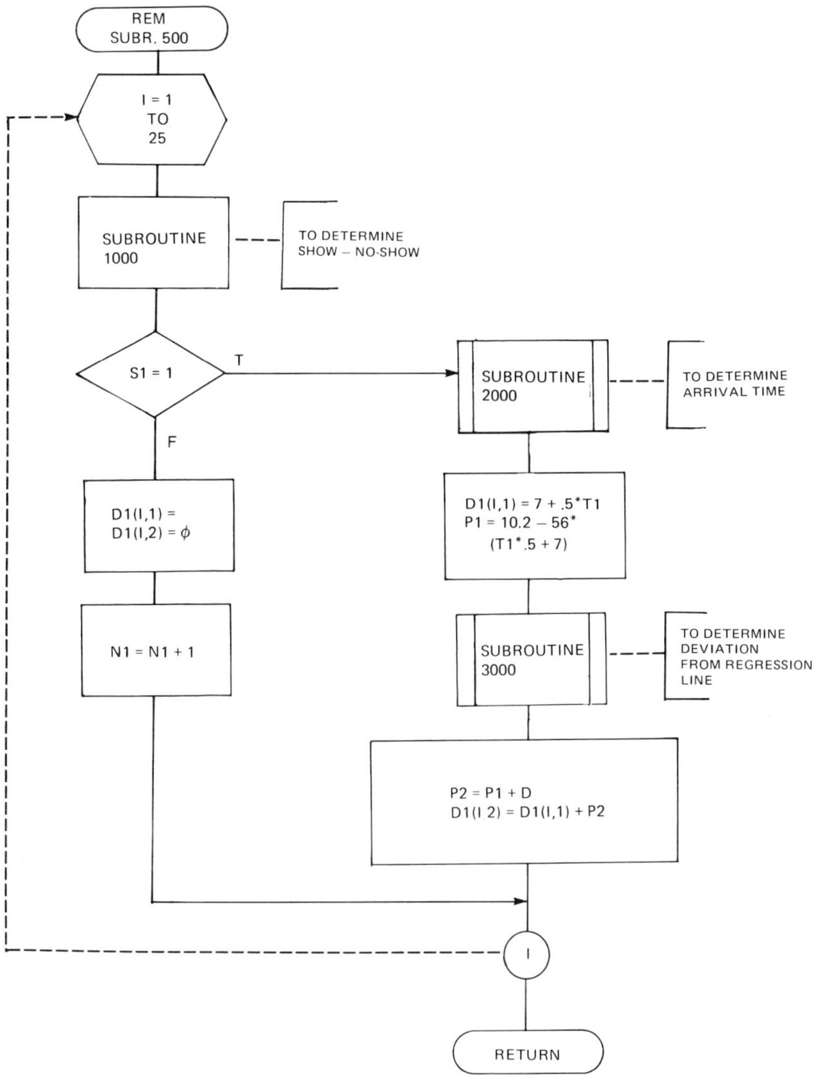
REM
SUBR. 500
I = 1
TO
25
SUBROUTINE
1000
TO DETERMINE
SHOW – NO-SHOW
S1 = 1
T
F
SUBROUTINE
2000
TO DETERMINE
ARRIVAL TIME
D1(I,1) =
D1(I,2) = ϕ
D1(I,1) = 7 + .5*T1
P1 = 10.2 – 56*
(T1*.5 + 7)
N1 = N1 + 1
SUBROUTINE
3000
TO DETERMINE
DEVIATION
FROM REGRESSION
LINE
P2 = P1 + D
D1(I 2) = D1(I,1) + P2
I
RETURN

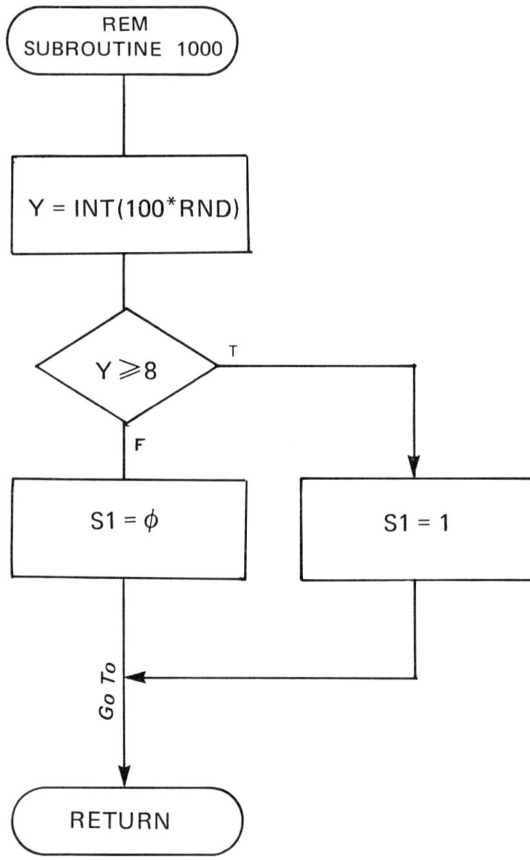
REM
SUBROUTINE 1000
Y = INT(100*RND)
Y ≥ 8
T
F
S1 = φ
S1 = 1
Go To
RETURN

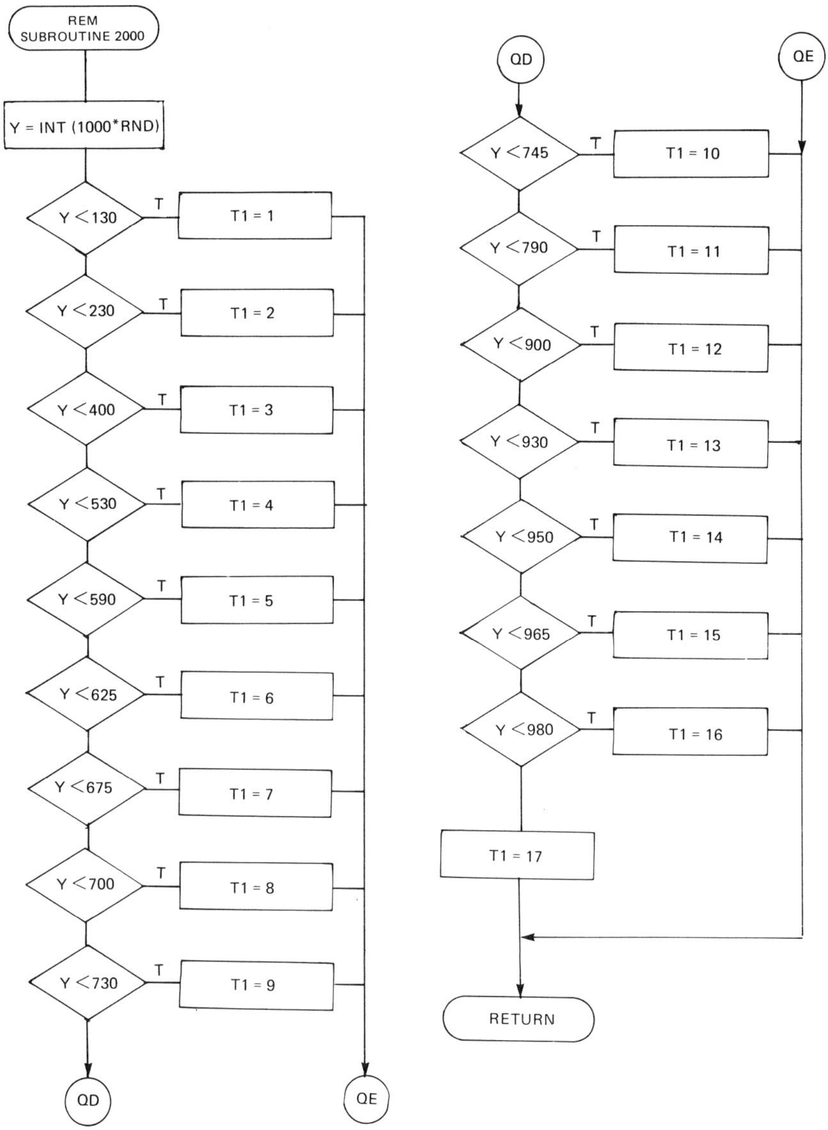
REM
SUBROUTINE 2000
Y = INT (1000*RND)
Y < 130
T
T1 = 1
Y < 230
T
T1 = 2
Y < 400
T
T1 = 3
Y < 530
T
T1 = 4
Y < 590
T
T1 = 5
Y < 625
T
T1 = 6
Y < 675
T
T1 = 7
Y < 700
T
T1 = 8
Y < 730
T
T1 = 9
QD
QE
QD
QE
Y < 745
T
T1 = 10
Y < 790
T
T1 = 11
Y < 900
T
T1 = 12
Y < 930
T
T1 = 13
Y < 950
T
T1 = 14
Y < 965
T
T1 = 15
Y < 980
T
T1 = 16
T1 = 17
RETURN

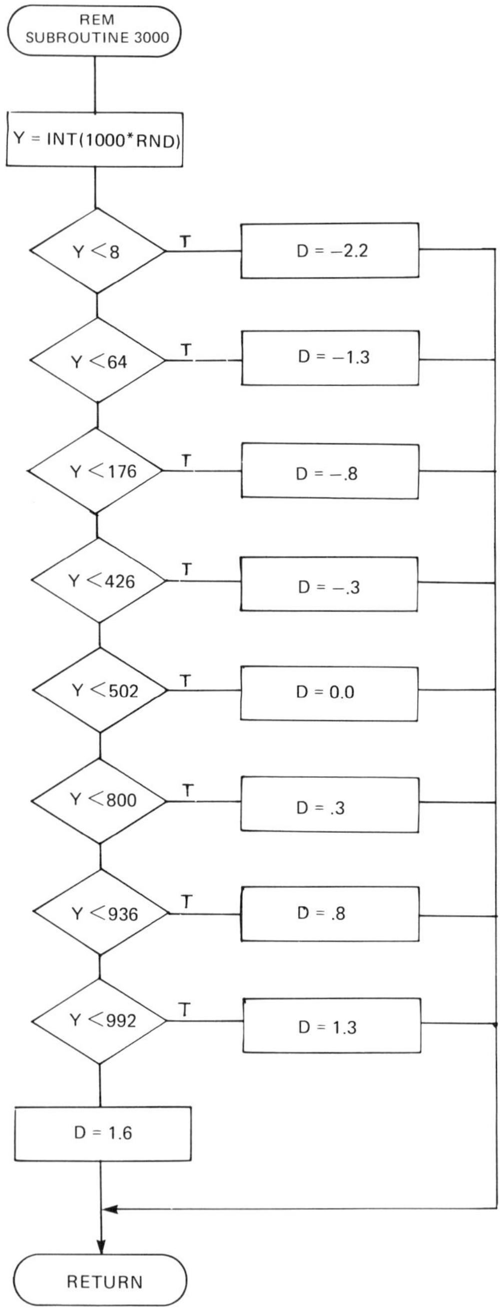
REM
SUBROUTINE 3000
Y = INT(1000*RND)
Y <8
T
D = −2.2
Y <64
T
D = −1.3
Y <176
T
D = −.8
Y <426
T
D = −.3
Y <502
T
D = 0.0
Y <800
T
D = .3
Y <936
T
D = .8
Y <992
T
D = 1.3
D = 1.6
RETURN

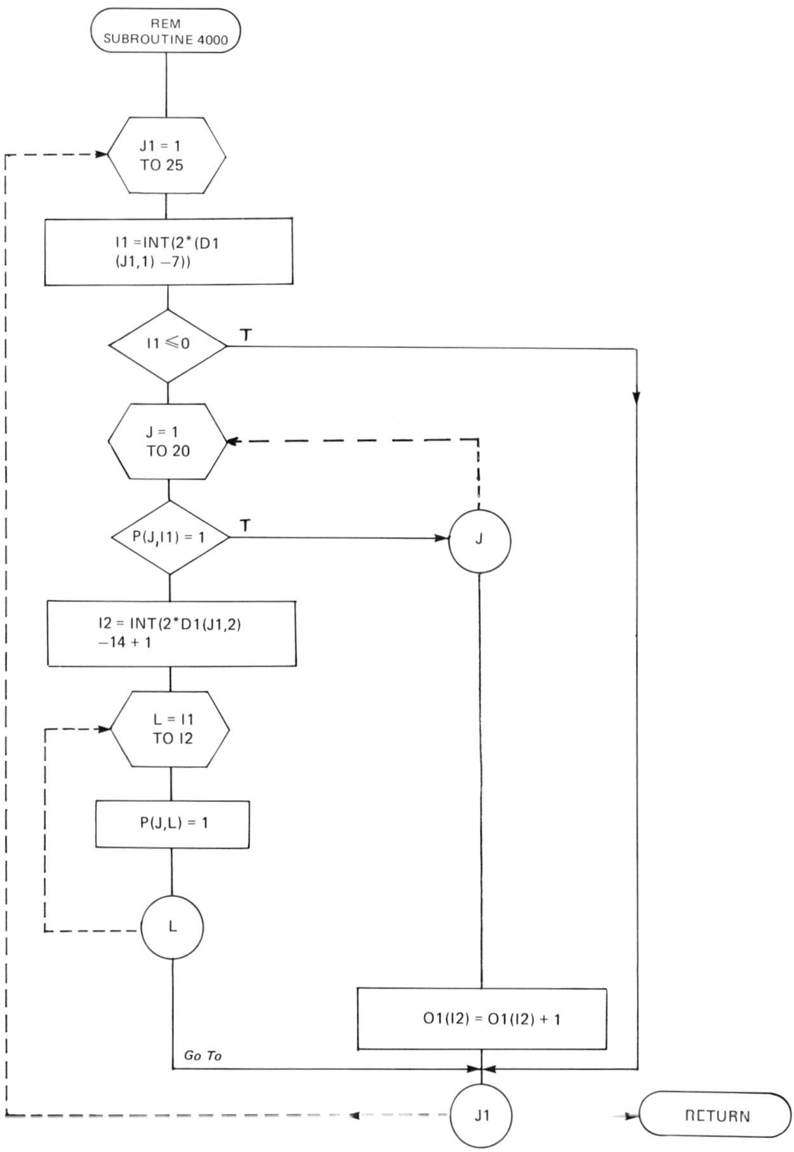
REM
SUBROUTINE 4000
J1 = 1
TO 25
I1 =INT(2*(D1
(J1,1) −7))
I1 ⩽0
T
J = 1
TO 20
P(J,I1) = 1
T
J
I2 = INT(2*D1(J1,2)
−14 + 1
L = I1
TO I2
P(J,L) = 1
L
O1(I2) = O1(I2) + 1
Go To
J1
RETURN

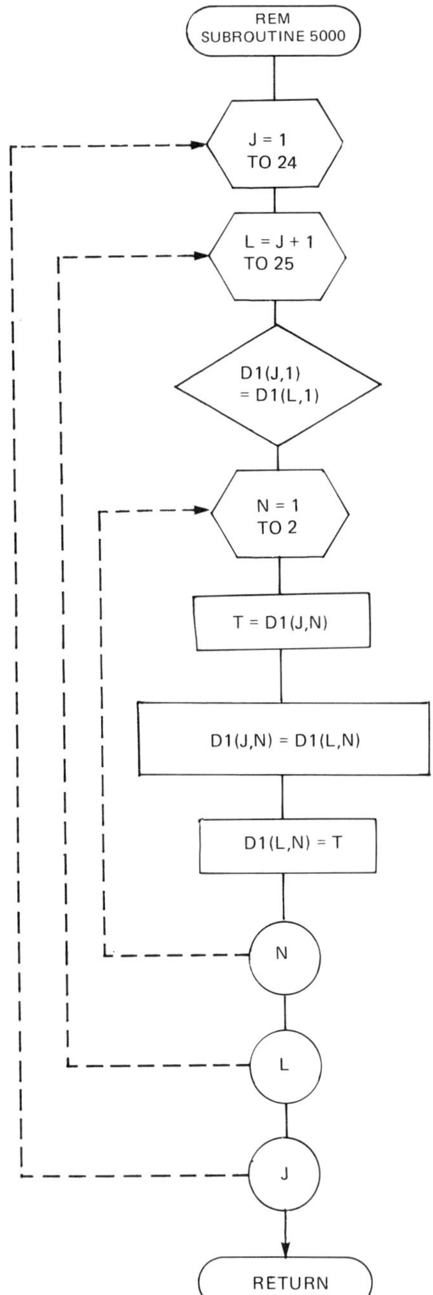
REM
SUBROUTINE 5000
J = 1
TO 24
L = J + 1
TO 25
D1(J,1)
= D1(L,1)
N = 1
TO 2
T = D1(J,N)
D1(J,N) = D1(L,N)
D1(L,N) = T
N
L
J
RETURN

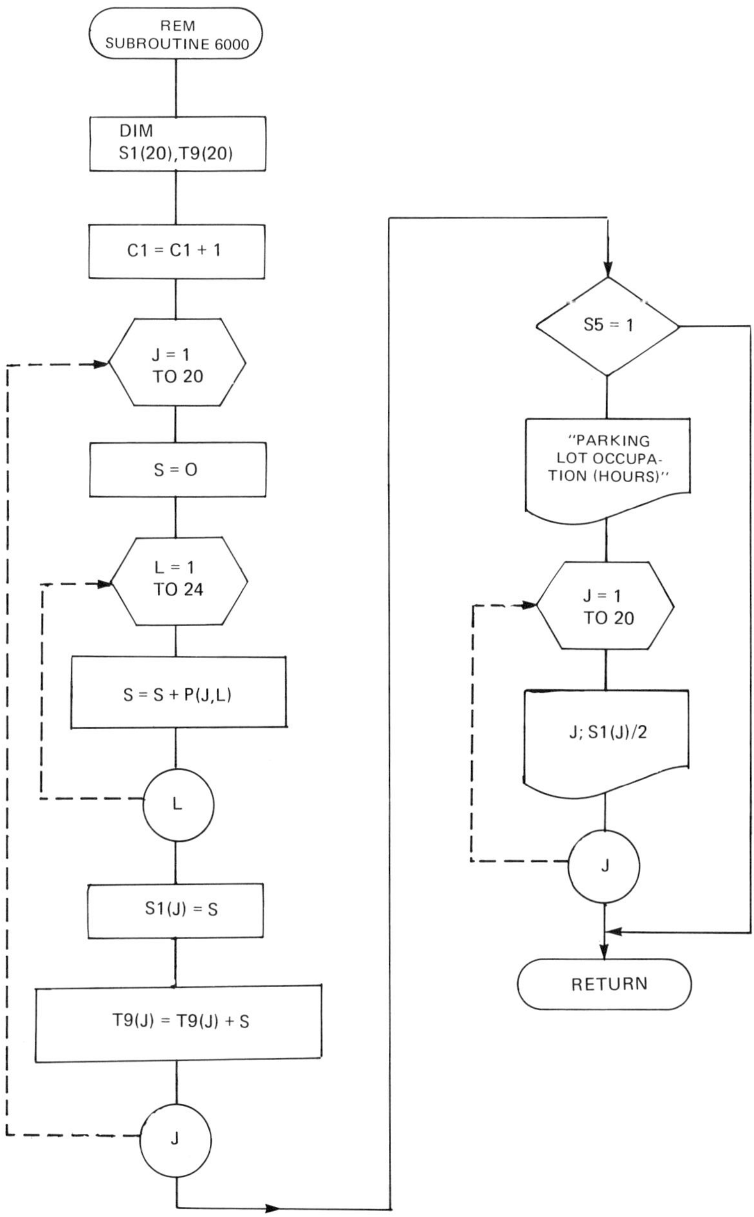

REM
SUBROUTINE 6000
DIM
S1(20),T9(20)
C1 = C1 + 1
J = 1
TO 20
S = O
L = 1
TO 24
S = S + P(J,L)
L
S1(J) = S
T9(J) = T9(J) + S
J
S5 = 1
"PARKING
LOT OCCUPA-
TION (HOURS)"
J = 1
TO 20
J; S1(J)/2
J
RETURN

Figure 8-16

The arrays in the program are defined as follows:

D1: driver array — shows arrival and departure time for each of the 25 drivers.

P: parking lot array — contains a 1 in element P(I,J) if a car is parked in parking slot I at time J.

01: counter for parking lot overflow — shows for each time slot (half hour period) how many cars have been unable to find a spot in the parking lot.

T9: counter for parking lot occupation — shows for each parking slot how many hours a day it has been occupied.

```
10   REM    PARKING LOT SIMULATION
20   REM
30   DIMENSION D1(25,2),P(20,24),01(24)
55   LET C1 = 0
57   LET N1 = 0
60   LET D2=1
61   MAT 01 = ZER
62   MAT T9 = ZER
65   FOR K = 1 TO 100
66   MAT P = ZER
100 GOSUB 500
221  GOSUB 5000
222  GOSUB 4000
227  LET D2 = D2 + 1
230  GOSUB 6000
240  NEXT K
245  PRINT "AVERAGE OCCUPATION"
247  PRINT "PARKING SLOT","HOURS"
250  FOR I = 1 TO 20
260  LET T9(I) = T9(I)/C1
270 PRINT USING 275, I, T9(I)/2
275 :###              ##.##
280  NEXT I
285  PRINT
290  PRINT "EXTRA SPACE NEEDED"
300 PRINT " TIME","NUMBER"
305  LET S = 0
310  FOR I = 1 TO 24
320 PRINT USING 322, 7+.5*I, 01(I)/100
322 :###.#             ##.##
325  LET S = S + 01(I)
330  NEXT I
335  PRINT
```

```
337 PRINT "ON THE AVERAGE DAY"
340 PRINT N1/100; " DRIVERS DID NOT SHOW"
345  PRINT
350  LET P7 = S/(2500 - N1)*100
360  PRINT P7; " PERCENT OF DRIVERS"
370  PRINT "DID NOT FIND A PARKING SLOT"
400  GO TO 9000
500 FOR I = 1 TO 25
510 GOSUB 1000
520 IF S1=1 THEN  560
530 LET D1(I,1) = D1(I,2) = 0
540 LET N1 = N1 + 1
550 GO TO 620
560 GOSUB 2000
570 LET D1(I,1)=7+.5*T1
580 LET P1=10.2 - .56*(T1*.5 + 7)
590 GOSUB 3000
600 LET P2 = P1+D
610 LET D1(I,2)=D1(I,1)+P2
620 NEXT I
630 RETURN
1000  REM  SUBROUTINE TO DETERMINE
1010  REM  SHOW-NO-SHOW
1020  REM
1030  LET Y = INT(100*RND)
1040  IF Y>=8 THEN 1070
1050  LET S1=0
1060  GO TO 1080
1070  LET S1=1
1080  RETURN
2000  REM  SUBROUTINE TO DETERMINE
2010  REM  ARRIVAL TIME
2020  REM
2030  LET Y=INT(1000*RND)
2040  IF Y<130 THEN 2200
2050  IF Y<230 THEN 2220
2060  IF Y<400 THEN 2240
2070  IF Y<530 THEN 2260
2080  IF Y<590 THEN 2280
2090  IF Y<625 THEN 2300
2100  IF Y < 675 THEN 2320
2102  IF Y < 700 THEN 2340
2104  IF Y < 730 THEN 2360
2110  IF Y < 745 THEN 2380
2120  IF Y < 790 THEN 2400
```

```
2130  IF Y < 900 THEN 2420
2140  IF Y < 930 THEN 2440
2150  IF Y < 950 THEN 2460
2160  IF Y < 965 THEN 2480
2170  IF Y < 980 THEN 2500
2180 LET T1=17
2190  GO TO 2510
2200  LET T1=1
2210  GO TO 2510
2220  LET T1=2
2230  GO TO 2510
2240  LET T1=3
2250  GO TO 2510
2260  LET T1=4
2270  GO TO 2510
2280  LET T1=5
2290  GO TO 2510
2300  LET T1=6
2310  GO TO 2510
2320  LET T1=7
2330  GO TO 2510
2340  LET T1=8
2350  GO TO 2510
2360  LET T1=9
2370  GO TO 2510
2380  LET T1=10
2390  GO TO 2510
2400  LET T1 = 11
2410  GO TO 2510
2420  LET T1 = 12
2430  GO TO 2510
2440  LET T1 = 13
2450  GO TO 2510
2460  LET T1 = 14
2470  GO TO 2510
2480  LET T1 = 15
2490  GO TO 2510
2500  LET T1 = 16
2510  RETURN
3000  REM  SUBROUTINE TO DETERMINE
3010  REM  DEVIATION FROM REGRESSION LINE
3020  REM
3030  LET Y=INT(1000*RND)
3040  IF Y<8 THEN 3140
3050  IF Y<64  THEN 3160
```

```
3060  IF Y<176  THEN 3180
3070  IF Y < 426 THEN 3200
3080  IF Y < 502  THEN 3220
3090  IF Y < 800 THEN 3240
3100  IF Y < 936 THEN 3260
3110  IF Y < 992 THEN 3280
3120  LET D=1.6
3130  GO TO 3290
3140  LET D=-2.2
3150  GO TO 3290
3160  LET D=-1.3
3170  GO TO 3290
3180  LET D=-.8
3190  GO TO 3290
3200  LET D = -.3
3210  GO TO 3290
3220 LET D = 0.0
3230  GO TO 3290
3240  LET D = .3
3250  GO TO 3290
3260  LET D = .8
3270  GO TO 3290
3280  LET D = 1.3
3290  RETURN
3950  REM
4000  REM  SUBROUTINE TO FILL
4010  REM  PARKING LOT
4020  REM
4025  FOR J1=1 TO 25
4030  LET I1 = INT (2*(D1(J1,1) - 7))
4035  IF I1 <= 0 THEN 4140
4040  FOR J = 1 TO 20
4050  IF P(J,I1) = 1 THEN 4110
4060  LET I2=INT(2*D1(J1,2)-14) + 1
4070  FOR L = I1 TO I2
4080  LET P(J,L) = 1
4090  NEXT L
4100  GO TO 4140
4110  NEXT J
4132  LET I2=D1(J1,1)
4134  LET O1(I2) = O1(I2) + 1
4140  NEXT J1
4150  RETURN
4990  REM
5000  REM  SORT BY ARRIVAL TIMES
```

```
5010  REM
5020  FOR J = 1 TO 24
5030  FOR L = J+1 TO 25
5040  IF D1(J,1) <= D1(L,1) THEN 5090
5045  FOR N = 1 TO 2
5050  LET T = D1(J,N)
5060  LET D1(J,N) = D1(L,N)
5070  LET D1(L,N) = T
5080  NEXT N
5090  NEXT L
5100  NEXT J
5110 RETURN
5120  REM
6000  REM
6010  REM      SUBROUTINE TO COMPILE
6020  REM       PARKINGLOT STATISTICS
6030  REM
6031  DIMENSION S1(20),T9(20)
6032  LET C1 = C1 + 1
6040  FOR J = 1 TO 20
6050  LET S = 0
6060  FOR L = 1 TO 24
6070  LET S = S + P(J,L)
6080  NEXT L
6090  LET S1(J) = S
6095  LET T9(J) = T9(J) + S
6100  NEXT J
6170  RETURN
9000  END
```

Figure 8-17

```
AVERAGE OCCUPATION
PARKING SLOT   HOURS
  1             8.84
  2             8.16
  3             7.75
  4             7.14
  5             7.01
  6             6.61
  7             6.51
  8             6.21
  9             6.21
```

```
 10              6.17
 11              5.92
 12              5.73
 13              5.54
 14              5.40
 15              5.14
 16              4.88
 17              4.55
 18              4.11
 19              3.47
 20              3.00

EXTRA SPACE NEEDED
 TIME           NUMBER
  7.5            0.00
  8.0            0.00
  8.5            0.00
  9.0            0.00
  9.5            0.00
 10.0            0.00
 10.5            0.00
 11.0            0.00
 11.5            0.00
 12.0            0.00
 12.5            0.02
 13.0            0.12
 13.5            0.96
 14.0            0.01
 14.5            0.00
 15.0            0.00
 15.5            0.00
 16.0            0.00
 16.5            0.00
 17.0            0.00
 17.5            0.00
 18.0            0.00
 18.5            0.00
 19.0            0.00

ON THE AVERAGE DAY
 1.97  DRIVERS DID NOT SHOW

 4.8198  PERCENT OF DRIVERS
DID NOT FIND A PARKING SLOT
```

Figure 8-18

This program is more complex than the others shown in this chapter. The reader is encouraged to study the flowcharts and coding carefully to gain an understanding of this program which uses several subroutines and the random number function to simulate arrivals and departures of 25 drivers over 100 days.

EXERCISES

1. Write a multiple-line user defined function to determine the sign of an integer N.
2. Use the function developed from problem 1. Write a program to read in X numbers and print out the numbers and their absolute values.
3. Write a subroutine that expresses a number as a product of prime numbers. For example, the number 350 has the factors 1, 2, 5, 5 and 7 (note that 5 appears twice).
4. Use the subroutine developed from problem 3 in an interactive program to find all the factors of any integer entered.
5. Consider the function
   $$f(x) = x^3 - 4x^2 + 3x + 3$$
   Write a program to find approximately where the function takes on the largest value over the interval of 0 to 2. Use .1 as the increment of the X values such that X = 0, X = .1, X = .2 and so on.
6. Construct a program to approximate the area under the curve
   $$f(x) = x^4 + 2x - 2$$
   on the interval [1, 3] using 10 subintervals.
7. Write a program using Newton's method for finding roots. Assume that XO is the initial guess for a root of f(X). Then an approximation for X1 can be expressed as:
   $$X1 = XO - \frac{f(XO)}{f'(XO)}$$
   Given that the function is:
   $$f(x) = x^4 + 2x - 3$$
   calculate and list six successive approximations to the root.
8. Write a program to compute the expansion of e^x

$$e^x = 1 + x + \frac{x^2}{2!} + \frac{x^3}{3!} + \ldots\ldots + \frac{x^n}{n!}$$

The general term is $\frac{x^n}{n!}$ (eg. $1 = \frac{x^0}{0!}$ and $x = \frac{x^1}{1!}$ etc.)

The terms are getting smaller and smaller, but n! itself is diverging and soon is greater than the limit of an integer. In this program it is sufficient to use n = 10. Use a multiple line function.

9. Write an interactive program to determine a prime number. Prepare a subroutine to determine whether or not a number N is prime. Then enter numbers via the INPUT statement.
10. Construct an interactive program to compute the material volume of a hollow sphere of thickness t. Let r be the radius of the nonhollow sphere. Prepare a subroutine to calculate the volume of a sphere which is defined as:

$$v = \frac{4}{3} \pi r^3$$

The volume of the material needed is

$$v = \frac{4}{3} \pi (r^3 - (r - t)^3)$$

9

File Processing

9.1 Introduction

Throughout the book we have focused on applications which require only small quantities of data which can be supplied either at the time the program is written (via the DATA statement) or at execution time (using the INPUT statement).

However, in many applications it is desirable to work with a larger data base. For example, in the parking lot example in chapter 8, the expected parking time was computed from a linear equation linking arrival time with parking time. In a real-world problem of this nature, the coefficients of this equation would be derived from observations, using the method of least squares. There might be many applications in an organization for a program to find regression coefficients, and the program might be used by several users. It would not be wise to have each user change the program by entering his own data; there is too much danger that somebody inadvertently destroys part of the program. It would not be an effective use of the computer to enter a large set of observations at execution time with the INPUT statement. Thus, there is a need to create a separate data file which can be linked to the program at execution time. In chapter 9, we will explain how data files can be created, read by a program, and written by a program. In section 9-5 we will give an example of a program to do simple linear regression; the procedure will be described at that time.

A file is a collection of related information. We are already familiar with one type of files — program files. Files can be stored on disk or tape, on punched cards, or even in folders in filing cabinets. In this chapter, we will be concerned with disk files only.

Files can be classified according to content: we can distinguish program files and data files. Files containing BASIC programs always have line (statement) numbers since BASIC requires this. Data files can have line numbers, but they are not required. Files can also be classified according to the access mode: sequential files are processed line after line in the order in which they are created, whereas records from a random access file can be read in any order. We will only discuss sequential files in this chapter; for information on random access files, check the manufacturer's manual for your installation.

9.2 Creating a Data File

Data files can be created using BASIC commands, or they can be written in a BASIC program. In this section, we will discuss file creation at the command level; writing data files in a BASIC program will be discussed in section 9.4.

Actually, the reader is already familiar with all the commands necessary to handle files; this was discussed for program files in chapter 1, and the same commands work for data files. Thus, only a short review is necessary at this time.

A new file is first created in core. This can be done in two ways:

1. type NEW filename.ext which clears memory and establishes the name filename.ext for the file to be created;
2. after entering BASIC with R BASIC and receiving a READY response, start typing. This will create a file called NONAME. Memory is not cleared.

With an interactive compiler, each statement is checked for syntax errors immediately after it has been typed in. This would result in an error message for data. Therefore, the command NO SYNTAX has to follow the NEW or R BASIC command.

Only data files with line numbers can be created using BASIC commands[1]. This is done by typing the line number, a space, and then the data separated by comma or spaces. Data files without line numbers can be created with editing programs, by copying data from cards into a disk file, or, in BASIC, with the PRINT # N statement discussed in section 9.4.

[1] With older compilers, it was possible to create data files without line numbers by simply starting the first data item at the beginning of the line, followed immediately by a comma and the next data item without embedded spaces.

Data files can contain both numerical and string values. It is not necessary to enclose string values in quotation marks if they start with a letter; it is, however, necessary to enclose numbers in quotation marks if they are to be read into a string variable.

Figure 9-1 shows an example of creating a data file with line numbers; figure 9-2 shows, for comparison, the same file without line numbers (created by an editing program).

```
PARK.DAT        11:26



100 8.50,6.15
200 7.30,7.05
300 7.75,4.95
400 8.05,5.07
500 10.00,5.00
600 11.45,3.75
700 15.80,1.03
800 14.00,3.12
900 12.00,5.07
1000 12.80,2.10
1100 9.60,4.83
```

Figure 9-1

```
NEW PARK.DAT

Ready
8.50,6.15
7.30,7.05
7.75,4.95
8.05,5.07
10.00,5.00
11.45,3.75
15.80,1.03
14.00,5.07
12.00,5.07
12.80,5.0
9.60,4.83
```

Figure 9-2

Once the file has been created in memory, it has to be stored on the disk so that it can be used later. In the case of a new file, this can be done with the SAVE command. If a file with the same name as used for the file in core already exists on disk, the SAVE command will result in an error message. In this case, the user has two options:

1. if the file stored on disk is no longer needed, type REPLACE instead of SAVE;
2. if the file on disk should be preserved, rename the file in core and then save it. The command to use is

RENAME ⟨filename.ext⟩

where filename.ext is the **new** name to be given to the file in core. Figure 9-3 illustrates the storing of a file on disk. The file in core is named PARK.DAT. The file is renamed to PARKWO.DAT Then a record is added. Again, the updated file cannot be saved. In this case, the REPLACE command is used.

```
SAVE

? Duplicate file name. REPLACE or RENAME
Ready
RENAME PARKWO.DAT

Ready
13.05,4.15
SAVE

? Duplicate file name. REPLACE or RENAME
Ready
REPLACE

Ready
```

Figure 9-3

What are the advantages of using line numbers in a disk file? Files are not always typed in perfectly, and mistakes may be detected after the file has been saved. In a file with line numbers, it is very easy to make changes: read the file into core using the OLD command, list it using the LIST command to see which lines need to be changed, and then type the line number and the correct data. Of course, the file has to be replaced at the end to preserve the changes.

Files without line numbers are required for certain statistical programs that are not written in BASIC. Also, files that are copied from cards or other data sources frequently do not have line numbers. It is possible to read and write these files in a BASIC program as will be discussed in the following sections. However, updating at the command level is only possible in very special cases; usually, a text editor is required to correct files without line numbers. It is beyond the scope of this book to discuss text editors.

9.3 Reading Files in BASIC

Three sets of statements are necessary to read data from disk files: statements to assign channels, to read the data, and to check for end of file.

9.3.1 Channel Assignments

BASIC is set up in such a way that nine input/output channels can be manipulated at the same time. For ease in management, these channels are numbered 1 through 9, and are assigned on a first-come basis — the first file to be handled is assigned to channel 1, etc. All input and output statements for files refer to these channel numbers.

However, files are stored on the disk under a filename which has been defined by the user. Thus, the channel number used in the program has to be linked to the disk file name. There are two statements in BASIC that can be used for this purpose — the FILES and FILE statement. Figure 9-4 illustrates the function of these statements.

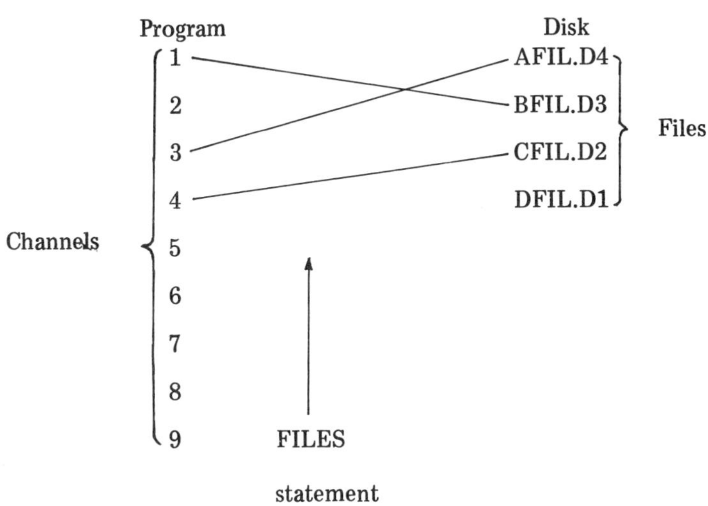

Figure 9-4

The format of the FILES statement is

n FILES ⟨filnam.ext, ... , filnam.ext⟩

where n is the statement number and filnam.ext is the name of an existing disk file.

For example, the assignments shown in figure 9-4 could be made using the statement

10 FILES BFIL.D3,,AFIL.D4, CFIL.D2

Note that the files are assigned to channels in the order in which they appear in the FILES statement: the file named first (BFIL.D3) is assigned to channel 1. Since no file name is listed between the first and second comma, channel 2 remains open. The remaining files are then assigned to channels 3 and 4.

The FILES statement is non-executable, which means that the assignments are made at compilation time and will not change during execution of the program.[1] A program may contain several FILES statements: these will be considered as one set of assignments. For example,

10 FILES A,B,C
100 FILES D,E,F

is equivalent to

10 FILES A,B,C,D,E,F

The FILES statement is appropriate when channel assignments need to be made only once and not more than nine channels are needed during program execution (which will generally be the case.)

For those cases when channel assignments need to be changed during program execution, an executable statement is available. Its general form is

n FILE argument 1,. . ., argument n

where n is the statement number and each argument assigns one channel to a file and has the form

\# N, ⟨string formula⟩

where N has a value between 1 and 9 (inclusive) and specifies the channel to be assigned, and string formula contains a file name and extension, enclosed in quotation marks. The quotation marks are required; the statement

300 FILE # 7, A . B

would lead to the error message

? ILLEGAL FORMULA IN LINE 300

The FILE and FILES statement can be used in the same program. A program outline involving both statements is shown below.

10 FILES INP.DAT,,UPDATE
20 } **read input data, perform computations**

[1]Since the statement is non-executable, it can be placed anywhere in the program.

```
990 IF IND=2 GO TO 2000
1000 FILE #1, "NEWFIL.E", #2, "UPMAS"
                                        } statements
                                        } to write
                                        } NEWFIL.E
2000 END
```

In this program, INP.DAT would be assigned to channel 1 and UPDATE to channel 3. After the computations have been performed, INP.DAT is no longer needed. Statement 1000 now assigns another file, NEWFIL.E, to channel 1 and also assigns UPMAS to channel 2 which has not been used previously.

If errors were detected during the computations, IND is set to 2, and the FILE statement will not be executed. Since the FILES statement is non-executable, IND.DAT and UPDATE will always be assigned to channels 1 and 3, regardless of what happens during program execution. If statement 1000 would read FILE #1, "INP.DAT" the contents of the file INP.DAT could be read a second time; in this case, the FILE works like a RESTORE statement.

9.3.2 Read Statements

After files have been assigned to channels, data can be read in from these files. Two input statements are available in BASIC, the READ # N and INPUT # N statements. The READ # N statement is used to read data files that have been created with line numbers, and the INPUT # statement is used for files that have been created without line numbers.

The general form of the READ # N statement is

n READ # N,<variable list>

where n is the statement number, N is the channel number, and variable list contains the names of the variables to be read in. The channel number N has to be defined in a FILES or FILE statement before the first READ # N statement is encountered.

For example, to read the information from the file PARK.DAT which was shown in figure 9-1, the following statements would be used:

```
10 FILES PARK.DAT
50 READ #1, A,B
```

Note that no variable name is provided for the line number. The READ # 1 statement indicates that the file has line numbers; therefore, they will simply be skipped when the statement is executed. The general form of the INPUT # N statement is

n INPUT # N, <variable list>

where n is the statement number, N is the channel number, and variable list contains the names of the variables to be read in. The channel number N has to be defined in a FILES or FILE statement before the first INPUT # N statement is encountered.

For example, to read the information from the file PARKWO.DAT which has been created in figure 9-2, the following statements would be used:

10 FILES PARKWO.DAT
50 INPUT # 1, A, B

There is no difference in the INPUT # N and READ # N statement as far as the program is concerned; they just apply to files created in two different ways. However, the two statements are **not** interchangeable. If the statement

60 READ # 1, A, B

is used with the FILES statement

10 FILES PARKWO.DAT

the error message

? BAD DATA IN LINE 60

will be printed.

9.3.3 End of File Check

After the last record created by the user, the system puts an end-of-file (EOF) record into each file. When the READ # N or INPUT # N is executed and an end-of-file is encountered, an error message

? EOF IN LINE n

is printed where n is the number of the statement being executed; after printing of this line, execution of the program stops.

As was discussed in chapter 5, the user will in most cases want to control what happens after the EOF is reached; summary statistics may need to be printed, records may need to be written to an output file, or, possibly, computations cannot even start until all the data have been read in. In chapter 5, two methods were discussed of preventing the program from stopping when the end of data is reached: count the number of records read or check for a trailer record.

A trailer record is automatically provided for disk files, namely the EOF. BASIC also has a statement to check for this trailer record, the IF END statement. This statement has the general form

n_1 IF END # N THEN n_2

or

n_1 IF END # N GO TO n_2

where n_1 is the number of the IF END statement, N is the channel number, and n_2 is the number of the statement to which control should pass after the EOF is reached.

If there is a chance that a file would be empty, the IF END # N statement should precede the first READ # N or INPUT # N statement. If files are not empty, the IF END # N statement can be placed after the READ # N or INPUT # N statement. In each case, the file is checked for EOF before a new record is read, and control is transferred when EOF is reached. Figure 9-5 shows an example using all the input statements discussed in this section.

Note: When the IF END statement is executed, the **next** record in the disk file is checked, not the record already read. Check carefully where the statement should be placed; it is possible to lose the last valid record if the IF END immediately follows the READ statement.

The FILES statement assigns PARK.DAT, a file with line numbers, to channel 1 and PARKWO.DAT, a file without line numbers, to channel 2. Statement 40 and 50 input data from PARK.DAT. The IF END statement is executed directly before the READ # 1 statement; after all the data have been read in, control is transferred to statement 90. Statements 90 through 100 refer to PARKWO.DAT. The statement block 90 through 130 is equivalent to statements 40 through 80, except that data are read from a file without line numbers.

The program simply computes the sum of the observations for each variable stored in the two files. By referring back to figures 9-1, 9-2, and 9-3, the reader can check that the program does exactly that.

9.4 Writing Files in BASIC

Two types of statements are needed to write files in BASIC: a statement that signals that the file is an output file, and the actual output statement.

9.4.1 The SCRATCH Statement

If not otherwise designated, a file is considered to be an input file. To create an output file, the SCRATCH statement is used. It has the general form

n SCRATCH #n_1 #n_2, . . .

where n is the statement number and n_1, n_2 are the channels assigned to output files. The SCRATCH statement must refer to at least one and at most nine channels.

Execution of the SCRATCH statement erases whatever may have been in the disk area allocated to the file and sets the file up in output mode. If an existing file is SCRATCHed, all information in that file is lost.

```
10 FILES PARK.DAT,PARKWO.DAT
20 LET S1=S2=0
30 LET T1=T2=0
40 IF END # 1 THEN 90
50 READ # 1,A,B
60 LET S1=S1+A
70 LET S2=S2+B
80 GO TO 40
90 IF END #2 THEN 140
100 INPUT #2,C,D
110 LET T1=T1+C
120 LET T2=T2+D
130 GO TO 90
140 PRINT S1,S2,T1,T2
150 END

Ready
RUN

FIG95           14:59



 117.25          48.12          130.3          57.
```

Figure 9-5

9.4.2 File Output Statements

After a file has been set up as an output file, either the WRITE # N or the PRINT # N statement can be used to enter data into the file. The general format of these statements is

n WRITE # N, <output list>

and

n PRINT # N, <output list>

where n is a statement number, N is the channel number assigned to the file, and output list can contain constants, variables, or expressions. Commas in the output list have the same effect as in the ordinary PRINT statement. Each number is written in a field of 14 characters; if the last item in the output list is a comma (e.g. PRINT #2,A,B,), the next execution of a PRINT # N statement will cause the data to be written into the **same** record.

If the WRITE # N statement is used, the file will be written **with** line numbers; the first record will be assigned number 1000, and subsequent line numbers will be in increments of 10. Each execution of the WRITE # N statement generates a new line number.

The PRINT # N statement generates records **without** line numbers, but functions in all other respects like the WRITE # N statement.

Figure 9-6 shows a program using all the file input/output statements. This program merges two files, AF and CF, which are sorted on record number (N and M, respectively). The updated file is written into BF, and the records that match are also written into file DF.

```
10 FILES AF,BF,CF,DF
20 SCRATCH #2, #4
25 LET C = 0
30 IF END #1 THEN 180
40 READ # 1,N,A,B
45 IF C > 0 THEN 70
50 IF END # 3 THEN 220
60 INPUT #3,M,E,D
70 IF N < M THEN 160
80 IF N = M THEN 110
90 WRITE #2,M,E,D
95 LET C = C + 1
100 GO TO 50
110 LET A = A + E
120 LET B = B + D
130 WRITE # 2,N,A,B
135 LET C = 0
140 PRINT #4,N; " UPDATED","A =";A;"B =";B
150 GO TO 30
160 WRITE #2,N,A,B
165 LET C = C + 1
170 GO TO 30
180 WRITE #2,M,E,D
```

Figure 9-6

Figure 9-6 (Con't)

```
190 IF END #3 THEN 260
200 INPUT #3,M,E,D
210 GO TO 180
220 WRITE #2,N,A,B
230 IF END #1 THEN 260
240 READ #1,N,A,B
250 GO TO 220
260 END

Ready
RUN

FIG96           10:18


Time:  0.13 secs.


Ready
OLD DF

Ready
LIST

DF              10:19

4  UPDATED   A = 51 B = 6

CF              10:19

2,17,24
4,36,16
5,-7,28

AF              10:20

10 1,20,30
20 4,15,-10
30 6,75,57
40 9,48,-2

BF              10:20

1000      1          20          30
1010      2          17          24
1020      4          51          6
1030      5         -7           28
1040      6          75          57
1050      9          48         -2
```

Files AF and BF have line numbers, as indicated by the READ #1 and WRITE #2 statements. Files CF and DF do not have line numbers as shown by the use of the INPUT #3 and PRINT #4 statements. The resulting output files are shown in figure 9-6.

Figure 9-7 summarizes the file input/output statements used in BASIC.

	File with Line Numbers	File without Line Numbers
Input statement	**READ # N**	**INPUT # N**
Check for EOF	**IF END # N THEN n**	**IF END # N THEN n**
Output statement	**WRITE # N**	**PRINT # N**
Set up for output	**SCRATCH # N**	**SCRATCH # N**
Assign channel (non-executable)	**FILES list**	**FILES list**
Assign channel (executable)	**FILE # N, filename**	**FILE # N, filename**

Figure 9-7

In the next section, a more extensive program using file statements will be discussed.

9.5 Regression Example

The example to be considered in this section is one of a simple linear regression. The purpose of simple linear regression is to fit a straight line to a set of n sample points (X,Y). The criterion for goodness of fit is to find coefficients a and b for a straight line $\hat{y} = a + bx$ such that $\Sigma(y-\hat{y})^2$ is a minimum, the so-called least-squares criterion. The process is illustrated graphically in figure 9-8.

To find coefficients **a** and **b** to minimize the sum of squares, the partial derivatives with respect to a and b are set to 0:

$$\frac{\delta SS}{\delta a} = -2 \sum_{i=1}^{n} (y - a - bx) = 0$$

$$\frac{\delta SS}{\delta b} = -2 \sum_{i=1}^{n} x(y - a - bx) = 0$$

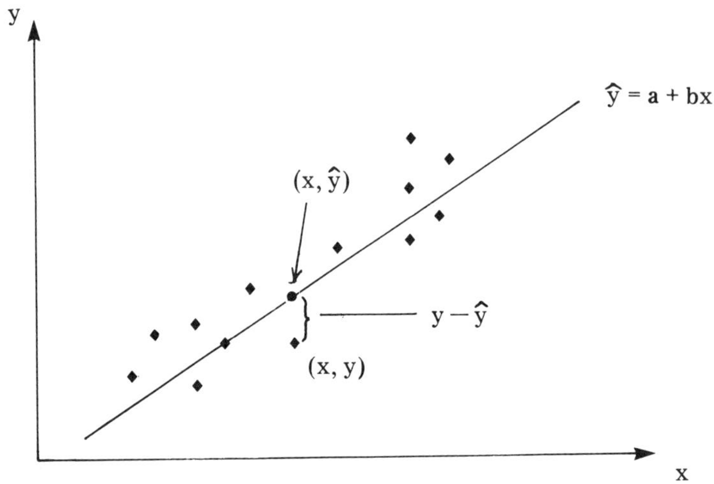

Figure 9-8

This leads to two linear equations in **a** and **b** which can be easily solved and yield the normal equations

$$b = \frac{n \sum_{i=1}^{n} x_i y_i - \sum_{i=1}^{n} x_i \sum_{i=1}^{n} y_i}{n \sum_{i=1}^{n} x_i^2 - \left(\sum_{i=1}^{n} x_i\right)^2}$$

$$a = \frac{1}{n} \sum_{i=1}^{n} y_i - \frac{1}{n} b \sum_{i=1}^{n} x_i$$

Figure 9-9 shows a program and sample printout for a simple linear regression. This is basically a straight-forward program, but a few comments may be helpful.

In applied problems, it is sometimes useful to perform statistical analyses on the residuals — the differences $Y - \hat{Y}$. Therefore, the program computes the residuals and writes them into a disk file which could then be used by another program at a later time. Thus, two files are assigned to channels 1 and 2 in statement 100, and the file RESID.DAT is declared as an output file in statement 200.

In order to compute the residuals, all observations must be stored in core until the coefficients have been computed, or they would have to be read twice. Statement 150 sets the program up to handle 100 observations. If an EOF is not read in the first 100 records, an error message is printed in lines 1900 and 2000, and the run continues with the first 100 records. The additional READ # 1 in line 1820 is issued in case exactly 100 observations are to be processed; in this case, the last READ # 1 statement would encounter an EOF, and processing continues. Reading 101 times in the loop would lead to an overflow for the arrays X and Y since 100 is set up as the largest subscript (see statement 150).

Statement 300 initializes all sums. In the loop (statements 1000 through 1800) the observations are read in, stored, and all sums that are required for the computation of **a** and **b** are accumulated. After all the data are read in, the coefficients are computed and printed in statements 2050 through 2600.

Finally, the residuals are computed and written into the residual file. A subroutine is used to compute the residuals to illustrate the use of subroutines. It is not necessary to do it this way, the simple computations could have been performed in the loop.

Figure 9-10 shows content of the residual file; note that the file is written with line numbers.

Finally, figure 9-11 shows a plot of the points in PARK.DAT and the regression line computed by the program.

```
100 FILES PARK.DAT,RESID.DAT
150 DIMENSION X(100),Y(100)
200 SCRATCH #2
300 LET S1=S2=S3=S4=0
340 REM
350 REM ************
360 REM S1 = SUM X
400 REM S2 = SUM Y
500 REM S3 =  SUM X*X
600 REM S4 = SUM X*Y
700 REM ************
800 REM
900 FOR I = 1 TO 100
1000 READ # 1,X1,Y1
1200 LET S1 = S1 + X1
1300 LET S2 = S2 + Y1
1400 LET S3 = S3 + X1*X1
```

```
1500 LET S4 = S4 + X1*Y1
1600 LET X(I) = X1
1700 LET Y(I) = Y1
1750 IF END # 1 THEN 2050
1800 NEXT I
1820 READ # 1 ,X1,Y1
1840 IF END # 1 THEN 2050
1900 PRINT "FILE TOO LARGE"
2000 PRINT "ONLY FIRST 100 OBSERVATIONS USED"
2050 LET N = I
2100 LET B = (N*S4 - S1*S2)/(N*S3-S1*S1)
2200 LET A = (S2 - B*S1)/N
2300 PRINT "INTERCEPT =" A
2400 PRINT "SLOPE = " B
2500 PRINT " _                _"
2600 PRINT USING 2700,S1/N,S2/N
2700 : X =#####.##  Y =#####.##
2800 REM
2900 REM  COMPUTE AND WRITE RESIDUALS
3000 REM
3100 FOR I = 1TO N
3200 GOSUB 4000
3300 WRITE # 2, X(I),Y(I),R
3400 NEXT I
3500 GO TO 5000
3600 REM
3700 REM SUBROUTINE TO COMPUTE RESIDUALS
3800 REM
4000 LET YO = A + B*X(I)
4100 LET R = Y(I) - YO
4200 RETURN
5000 END

Ready

RUN

REGRES          15:21


INTERCEPT = 10.3014
SLOPE = -0.556036
 _          _
 X =   10.66  Y =     4.37
```

Figure 9-9

```
RESID.DAT     10:12

1000    8.5      6.15     0.574923
1010    7.3      7.05     0.807681
1020    7.75     4.95    -1.0421
1030    8.05     5.07    -0.755293
1040    10       5        0.258977
1050    11.45    3.75    -0.184772
1060    15.8     1.03    -0.486017
1070    14       3.12     0.603119
1080    12       5.07     1.44105
1090    12.8     2.1     -1.08412
1100    9.6      4.83    -0.133438

Ready
```

Figure 9-10

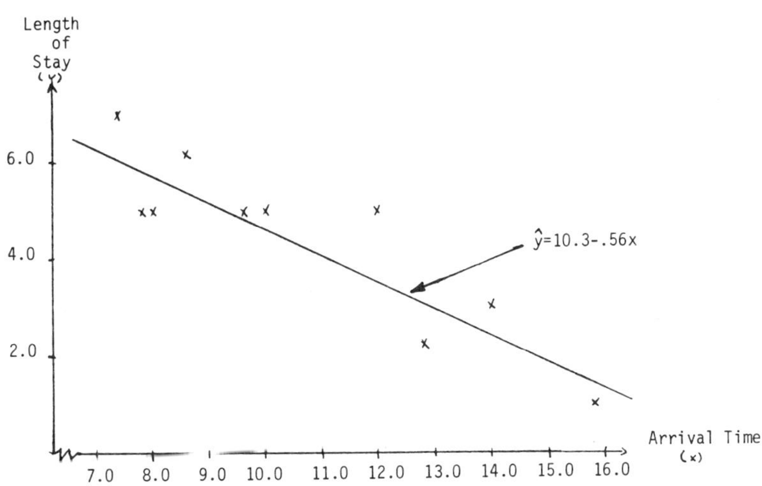

Figure 9-11

EXERCISES

1. Examine the following program segments. Identify the files as input or output files; files with line numbers or without line numbers; or not possible to identify.

   a.
   ```
   10 FILES ANGLE.P1,DISTAN.P1
   20 SCRATCH #2
   30 WRITE #2,D
   ```

   b.
   ```
   50 FILES RAD1.P2,,VOLU.P2
   60 SCRATCH #3
   70 INPUT #1, R
   80 WRITE #3, V
   ```

   c.
   ```
   100 FILES ABCD.IN,EFGH.OUT
   110 SCRATCH #2
   120 READ #1,A,B,C,D
   180 PRINT #2,E,F,G,H
   190 IF END #1 THEN 290
   ```

   d.
   ```
   200 FILE #4, "INDAT.P3"
   210 READ #4,A3,B3
   220 FILE #6, "OUTDAT.P3"
   280 SCRATCH #6
   290 WRITE #6,"INDAT.P4"
   ```

2. Identify and correct errors, if any, in the following programs.

   a.
   ```
   100 REM ACCESSING FILES
   110 FILES INPUTF.P1, OUPUT.P1
   120 SCRATCH 2
   130 READ 1, X,Y
   150 END
   ```

   b.
   ```
   200  FILES FILE1, FILE2
   210  INPUT #1,X,Y
   220  SCRATCH #1,X,Y
   230  LET Z=(X+Y)/2
   240  PRINT  #1,X,Y,Z
   250  IF END #1 GO TO 290
   260  GO TO 210
   290  END
   ```

c.
```
300 FILES FILE3,,FILE5
310 SCRATCH #3
320 READ #1,X,Y
330 IF END #3, THEN 370
340 LET Z=(X 2 + Y 2)/2
350 PRINT 3,X,Y,Z
360 GO TO 320
370 PRINT "PROCESSING IS COMPLETED"
380 END
```

Programming Problems

1. Create a random number file that contains 30 random integers between 1 and 100. Be sure that line numbers exist in the file.
2. Write a program to access the file created from problem 1 above. Separate the numbers into 2 sets, one consists of even numbers and the other consists of odd numbers. Finally, write two output files; one consists of odd numbers, the other contains even numbers.
3. Do the same calculations as in problem 2 but write the files without line numbers.
4. Write a program to access the even number file. Calculate and print the range of that file.

Index